CIRCLE OF ONE

Messages from the animals
of the
Hacienda de los Milagros,
a teaching and healing sanctuary.

Hacienda de los Milagros
3731 North Road One West
Chino Valley, AZ
U.S.A. 86323
928-636-5348 • Cell 928-533-0684
hdlmsanctuary.org

Cover Art: Circle of One, Acrylic, 2009
Donated by: Liz Nicholas, Art With A Conscience, liznicholas.com
Book Design: Allisone PrintGraphics, Prescott, AZ

DEDICATION

To humans,
Be wise and loving to everyone,
and be sure to include yourself.
With love from,
The Milagros

TABLE OF CONTENTS

FOREWORD

By the end of the 20th century, human science had made the amazing discovery that the animals around us live deeply emotional lives, so much so that we must consider the fact that they have souls in the spiritual sense. This revelation forms the beginning of new kinds of relationships for all sentient beings, relationships that can lead from awareness to enlightenment.

In walking among the horses and the nearly 100 burros at Hacienda de los Milagros, Pat and I felt no fear. A calmness came over us not unlike meditation. It was an effortless meditation that opened our hearts to the many hearts of four-legged compassion. The sweetness of it brought tears to our eyes. We were both giving and receiving in the same moments of joy.

We were surrounded by empathetic souls who freed us from all judgments and all fears. The quality of acceptance came in every touch, and in eye contacts the gift of understanding was immediately accessible. It was a wonderful experience that all master teachers recommend to us... the end of separation... the ultimate recognition that all life is sacred.

Thank you, dear human and animal friends, for demonstrating the most important lesson of life: we are all family.

A great Sufi master and poet, Hafiz, who lived in the 14th century, wrote I Have Learned So Much (translated by Daniel Ladinsky). The words seem to resonate with our experience at the sanctuary.

I

Have Learned

So much from God

That I can no longer

Call

Myself

A Christian, a Hindu, a Muslim,

A Buddhist, a Jew

i

The Truth has shared so much of Itself
With Me
That I can no longer call myself
A man, a woman, an angel
Or even pure
Soul

Love has
Befriended Hafiz so completely
It has turned to ash
And freed
Me
Of every concept and image
My mind has ever known.

Monty Joynes

PREFACE

Welcome. You have been guided here. Your heart has guided you here. If you do not already have direct experience with animals in this capacity, there is part of you that desires to awaken. A part of you desires to awaken to the understanding that animals are much more than they appear. They are much, much more than most on this planet believe. A part of you knows this.

There will be some who will scoff that the animals we share the earth with have important things to share and that they communicate with those willing to listen. Certainly, in their minds they will be correct; their minds are closed to the possibility. It is not, however, the mind that these words speak to. The messages within these pages, given from the hearts of the animals, speak to the heart within. It is with your heart that the animals want to connect. If you listen with your heart, the animals say, you will hear them.

The beings from Hacienda de los Milagros are not out of the ordinary; they are not special. They have just had the opportunity to share. Wisdom, these ones would say, is within every animal on the planet. They would share that each animal, from animal companion to wild species, has thoughts, feelings, and emotions. And a soul. The animals at this Home of Miracles would certainly encourage you to listen to every individual animal-being, as each has a unique life, love, experience, and perspective. They would also say that it is easy when you know how, or more precisely, when you remember how.

This book is a result of a great effort by many who volunteered their time. Each animal communicator who donated their skills did so because they believe the animals have something important to share, and wanted to help them share it. Whether you believe these messages come from animals is not important. What is important is to read them with your mind open. If your mind is open, then the heart can hear. That is really all the animals ask of you. Besides, when wisdom is gifted, does it really matter from where it comes?

Many thanks to those who have contributed their time into making this book a reality. Their love for the animals created this book. A very special thank you to Liz Nicholas who painted and donated the magnificent artwork that adorns this cover. Special gratitude to all of the animal communicators who heard the call for assistance and gave of themselves to take down messages. Every gracious one is listed at the back of this book. Thank you. And a personal thank you to Edwin, my heart, who works hard so that I get to play.

It has been my profound privilege to bring these messages all together; it has not been without tremendous inner growth. The animals, if you are open, have a way of illuminating your inner world and sparking growth for you. In the experience of many, there are furred, feathered, finned and scaled masters among them.

The greatest and grandest gratitude goes to the animals of Hacienda de los Milagros for sharing who they really are. They have now shared their voices, as was their request, undoubtedly with more wisdom to come. We have kept their delightful and special way of sharing, phrasing, and spelling intact.

We asked of each animal-being the same question:
"Do you have anything you would like to share with humans?"

Do you have a heart to hear?

-Sue Manley

INTRODUCTION

I have been blessed with many friends who communicate. Many of them received some of the messages that follow, and they will also be thanked later. There are powerful beings living here, and yet they are simply representative of all of creation. The non-human animals residing with you would tell you the same things. They never judge us, and they love us and wait for us to rejoin the rest of creation.

I'd suggest you might want to have some tissues handy, for happy and joyful tears, not tears of sadness. I still need them when I read these and feel the unconditional love that they flow from. Maybe our non-human friends don't have ego, or maybe they have it well in hand. They would like us to become aware of what we are doing, and change, before we destroy more life. These incredibly powerful messages will guide humans to a more aware existence, learning how to share the unconditional love of ALL creation. You will feel these gifts of love and energy into your very soul. All of these beings are my soul brothers and sisters.

If you like what you read, please consider helping us continue our mission at the sanctuary. Our Vision Statement, which came from our residents and higher source, is included. But first, please read what my brothers and sisters have to say. Read, learn, expand, and enjoy.

Many humans have provided unconditional love, support, encouragement and lessons.

Barbara Metzger, co-founder of the sanctuary, without who this would have been much more difficult.

Jeri Ryan, Ph.D. (Auntie Jeri) who gave me the encouragement and help to begin more actively to open up and realize my own communication skills.

Sister Janice Goff, who would not let me stop or ignore or plead inability;

Sister Sue Manley, without who this book may not have ever been finished, and who kept me, as much as is possible, on the path and steering me away from self-doubt;

Sister Beverly McLean, who helped keep energies balanced and everyone in good health with her incredible energy work and natural medicine talents;

Sister Christina Montana, who helped especially when we faced the possibility of closure and asked the tough questions of our residents when I simply could not due to my emotional connections with the past, present and future residents;

Sister Danielle Tremblay who along with Christina continue to work with the residents;

Sister Deborah Derr, D.C. founder of United in Light, an incredible draft horse retirement sanctuary in Livingston, Montana, who helped me deal with my issues and supported the residents in so many ways.

And, of course, the residents, particularly my Sister Clover, who, with rest of The Council of the Animals, is always with us, supporting us, giving us advice and moral support in every thing we do at HDLM. if we but ask. We are truly blessed to be under the wings of The Council.

We have a huge mission, all of us. To be part of all this, and to help facilitate the incredible changes coming to our Earth, has been, continues to be, and will continue to be an honor of immense and incredible magnitude.

Feel their love, and please join us!

– Wynne Zaugg

When I co-founded Hacienda de los Milagros, Inc., I could never have imagined the adventure that it would be.

It was such an honor and blessing to love and take care of the animals that resided at the sanctuary, and I am forever grateful to each and every one of them. These four-legged souls taught me so much.

They are forever in my heart. We learned about animal communication early in the creation of the sanctuary and with it, everything changed. We gave it a try with the help of an experienced animal communicator, asking a new four-legged friend what they would like to be called.

There was something so different about calling an animal by a name they had chosen. It totally changed the way I looked at animals and every living thing. There was a deeper connection that went far beyond the physical. And most importantly, there was mutual respect. I didn't see them anymore as a helpless yet cute animal.

I saw them as a powerful, independent soul. The animals seemed so open to communicate, like they had been patiently waiting. And they probably had been waiting as this is simply the way it should be. To see them respond to the communication was incomprehensible and awesome at the same time. They just blossomed!

I am so grateful to the animal communicators that helped us over the years talk with our residents. With their help it progressed to asking each new resident how they were feeling, to asking them if they had a message they would share with people. This book is their gift to us. I've always felt that it's not so hard to believe in telepathic communication with animals. It's much harder to 'hear' the communication from our four-legged friends. My hope is that as you read these messages, you'll 'hear' them with an open heart, and then live with them with a heightened awareness and love for all souls. Always remembering that we are connected to all living things, there is only one. Just as these messages were given to us. From that spirit of oneness and with love.

-Barbara Metzger

MESSAGES

ABBEY, HORSE, MARE

Take a look around

Try to see what I see

I see you looking, but not seeing

I see you thinking, but not feeling

I see you walking, but not flying

I see you, do you see me?

ABBY, BURRO, JENNY

I would like to tell humans that it is nice of them to look after us. I would like to tell them that if it were up to me, I would prefer to live how our ancestors lived, out in the wild and free. That is something that humans should know. We have not always been "cared for", you know. There once was a time when we cared for ourselves. And we loved it! We were free. We were living our own lives and were very successful. Humans think they know everything. But they do not. We have lots to share with them. They only need to be quiet and listen.

Their hearts speak the same language as our hearts. Our hearts are here. Sometimes, human hearts are not. Sometimes, humans can't feel them. I would wish that for you humans. To feel your hearts. That would be a great wish for them if they could do that. I don't know why many can't. I wish that for them for sure. Then they will be free. Like we are. I know, our bodies are not free, but our hearts are. And that is the most important. Hearts are most important. And I like mine. I live through it every day. I wish for humans to live through their hearts every day.

–SM

ABIGAIL, BURRO, JENNY

Well, to be a human is a wonderment. I think humans always have wonderments. And good for them! It makes things happen to have wonderments. Because one wonderment leads to another and pretty soon we have a big understanding and that's very, very good.

I don't have to be human to have wonderments. I have them every single day almost all day long - except when I want to be only in my heart and in myself. Then I turn off my wonderments, wondrous though they may be. I can always find them again or better ones if I'm done with the first ones and don't know it.

So wonderment calls for just noticing, paying attention and noticing little things that sometimes go ignored. And realizing that wonderment of little things can make big things happen. So I never think that my wonderments are too small. In fact, the small ones can give bigger feelings than the big ones because the small ones are so full of meaning. So are the big ones. But sometimes the meaning gets lost in the complexity and we spend all our time figuring out the complexity and then wonderment goes by the wayside.

I think it's important to love and encourage your wonderments no matter how big or small they are. And don't let the small ones get lost in the wake of the big ones. And don't let the big ones fall apart and get fragmented by focusing on all the little ones that are in the big one.

Let me catch my breath. I think that's all. Can you imagine what the world would be like without wonderments? Please don't let that happen.

–SM

ABUELO, BURRO, JACK

My message is one of sadness and appreciation. So sad for all of those who died. Sad for the cruelty in the world, the fear. Sad for the world and this cruelty and for the damage it does. Sad for the sadness in so many hearts and the fear that makes such big mistakes like this one (the capture and removal from Death Valley National Park).

I appreciated the care and the trouble and the goodness in many hearts who helped us and continue to do so. My heart thanks you. My heart wants to help. I can only be here and send thank yous to all those good ones and ask that you continue to give with your hearts so the goodness grows.

–JR

ABUELO AMARANTES MILAGRO
BURRO, JACK (IN SPIRIT)

Our good friend Janice Goff had the following conversation with Abuelo following his departure. It is especially interesting to me because I got a message the morning after his departure that one of the things he was here for was to have a more positive relationship with a human than he had had before in previous lifetimes.

Janice: *Will you visit the burros in Death Valley? (to let them know about his year's rescue and to let them know that there is nothing to fear.)*

Abuelo: As we speak I have run with the herd.

Janice: *I was to further understand that he is a mediator with this concern. He will be present at the gathering presenting/bridging both sides.*

Will you share your experience of death?

Abuelo: Walking from one pasture to another through a gate.

Janice: *Would you be willing to tell me more about this?*

Abuelo: When spirit and death meet... it is the gate. When spirit and birth meet... it is the gate. It is the same experience.

Janice: *Did you learn anything going through the gate or simply go through?*

Abuelo: It is where true self is realized. Self free of all restrictions. It is where you see how you have lived your life. I did not live my life waiting to die. I saw that here. I lived my life to be a life each day. There is nothing here for the mind to busy itself with. The mind sleeps. The true self is realized.

Janice: *What do you want to leave with Barb & Wynne?*

Abuelo: I saw each day of my life there their coming and going... their constant movement in and out, to and from, back and forth. Many times a day I saw this. I watched them and watched them. I tried in the beginning to only watch them. Then I began to watch to understand why. Why would they go through this monotonous ritual every every every day! The sun would rise and there they were. The sun at mid-day and they were there.

The sun would set and they were there. Day after day. I was a well-known person all of my human lives (and well known in all of the others). And they (Barb & Wynne) attended each day just like all the people that worked for me, and for good reason...Greed. We all worked each day to squeeze the life out of it or should I say squeeze the money out of each day...every day. Every day. At my beck and call to do my bidding. I remember the day I got bored with watching them. This was nonsense!!!! I know, because I was a part of the whole scenario that no one was paying them anything to attend to our needs, because I wasn't. I couldn't figure it out. I hung my head and just stood there. I heard footsteps...

I looked up just a little and Wynne stood there. He was looking me over so I looked him over. I don't know what I looked like in this big body except by what everybody else looked like around me. Then he reached out and touched me. He sighed. And I felt his heart heave. That's the first time I <u>EVER</u> wept from my heart. He loved me. He didn't know what's been going on in my head, and maybe he did. But he loved me. I started to live again. Every day. Sunrise to sunset. And not live to die. They gave me the sanctity of life. It was a miracle.

–JG

ADOBE SUN, HORSE, GELDING

Humans are like horses who chase their tails. Humans go round and round again without coming up for air sometimes when presented with problems and conflict.

When a horse is in trouble we either take charge of the situation or flee. One decision is no nobler than the other.

You humans debate and figure out and instead of letting your heart, (which should be instinctual for you), lead you, you get all wrapped up and tied amongst yourselves. You have a hard time figuring each other out, let alone yourselves.

I would encourage you to look at your problems from a new perspective. Horses stand back and look at things we are unaccustomed to from a distance. We would encourage you to distance yourself from the problem so you have a better view.

How do you do that? Simple. Let your thoughts guide you to a sit down position with your body. Take a time out. Don't engage with the problem. View it from the side. Treat it like a spectacle you are watching rather than being the competitor within the game. If you take a wider viewpoint you will find the conflict is not nearly as bad as you thought and the problem will be lighter

With this newfound perspective you can flee quicker or deal with it head-on, like we do. It's a noble thing to know how to respond to a problem without getting all caught up in the quagmire of it all. Don't get yourselves stuck. Freedom of thought comes from being unstuck in life.

Being unstuck means fewer perceived problems. Few problems mean greater enjoyment of life.

–DT

AHIMSA, BURRO, JENNY

First I'd like to say you as a human lot have come a long way. We are no longer in the dark ages where animals were seen as burdens or even as builders, for that matter! Today's doings show a greater aptitude or awareness for that which exists around you.

Today you look at the sky and may see a rain cloud, but there is more beyond and you're near the brim of witnessing that as well. Let me speak more plainly here.

There is a great deal each one of us must do to benefit the whole. Can't you see where the morning star rises? It's high above by noon and then sets low in the galaxy. We are like those morning stars.

Each of our comings and goings is celestial in nature and of all importance. I am one with you and you are one with me, despite appearances. We are like clones, you might say, in regards to our natural origin. We are not as different as you think (she laughs).

Our work here is to help you understand this lack of separation that many people still lay claim to. We are each doing that in our own way. The powerfulness of one is the powerfulness of many and yet it is the same.

You should see the heavens from afar. The differences are so few. So few as to really count. Each one of us is a being beyond compare and

Ahimsa with Baby Zach, photo by Deb Derr

6

because we are all dwelling within this awesome prosperity of our time we are here to witness it.

You too will see the emerging of a new society of peoples. You will come out of the dark, to play with us wee ones and never bat an eye or look at us as you did back in the 'dark ages' of the time that is currently your present. You will expand and go ever present into the future.

The 'dark ages' are like time slipping away. The horizon is new and fresh and a bit beyond us, yet attainable for everyone. This is my message. Danielle: Is there anything else you'd like to share?

Just one thing, the people who surround their doings and me are helping light the candle. It is they, amongst many, who are lifting the night-shade to welcome in the dawning hour. They are not alone in their work certainly. But they are one among many. It is my purpose to express that. As they see me, I say it as much. Thank you.

–DT

AHIMSA, BURRO, GELDING (IN SPIRIT)

We here in the spirit world are closer to you than you think. For some we are the gentle flow of air along your ear, the shadow in your room that calms and protects you, the lights flickering at night, the pulling of your ear, or the thought that enters your head at just the right moment.

Do not fear us for we are what you call Angels, we are those answers to your tears. We also ask that you send us your tears of joy, love and happiness. For once you acknowledge these things your world will change. Give thanks to all, for All gives thanks to you.

–S

7

AHNA GAY, BURRO, JENNY

Humans would do well to listen to themselves more, listen to themselves speak. They tend to talk, but do not listen to what they are really trying to say. It is like manifesting their destiny if they speak with clarity. This they should know. They would do well to do this very act and their lives would open up accordingly... their lives would open up to what they wish them to be. They can manifest their wants, needs, desires... whatever it is they would like, if they would only listen to what comes out of their mouths and that which is in their hearts. This I know for sure.

Also, humans could always do well to laugh at themselves more -- they tend to take themselves very seriously in this life -- look at us, we rest and relax. We work when we have to... when it is time. But there is time for rest and time always for laughter. Thank all those ones with whom you have contact, for they share their blessings with you, they share part of themselves with you and this is a gift. We are many and have many gifts. We share with each other. All are one within this realm of ours. All are one in this living we do.

Humans have separated themselves far too much. They see themselves as individuals and not part of the whole. This is not a correct way of viewing things. We are all one. We are all alive to assist one another and to live the plans of our lives. This is what we do. Tell humans they waste too much time being alone in their thoughts, alone in the way they do things, alone in their hearts. Reach out and feel the hearts of all. The hearts of all are connected to the one and this is what I desire humans to know. This is very important. Humans should not be alone in their hearts.

We are here to assist in the transition that is happening across the world -- the transition of bringing in love and respect and reverence for all beings -- we are all one. We assist in this by being who we are, by being one with each other and one with those of open heart. All those who have open hearts will hear. It is to humans' detriment that they have closed themselves, their hearts down. We assist by opening up people's hearts when they view our bodies, when they feel our love, when they know we are friends. This I know. This is very important.

Please tell humans to love one another. Please tell them it is important to respect those of different species. We may look different, but we are not... we are all one in spirit and will all go to the same place when our bodies are finished with this earth. We are one. This is important. We assist humans by maintaining our heart centers. This gives them a chance to remember... it is like a tuning fork. Those with hearts ready to be opened can feel our love and this will attune them to greater opening. We are love. We know this and this is important. Thank you for speaking with me this day. Kindness to you and those you love. Kindness to all.

–SM

ALBIREO, HORSE, MARE

I am a jammin' horse.
When I move, I'm dancin' to the star beat.
Hoof-dee-hoof-dee-hoof!
Can you hear it?
We're all dancin' to a bigger beat.
Hoof-hoof-hoof-dee-hoof!
Can you keep up with me?
The world is a spinnin'
Hoof-hoof-dee-bop-dee-hoof-dee-bop-dee-bop!
Lift your hooves, peoples.
Ride on a sunbeam.
Ride the moonbeam.
Pick up the pace.
Move to the star beat.
Whinnies with happiness!
Hoof-dee-hoof-dee-hoof-dee-bop!
Whinneeeeeee
–CM

ALICE, BURRO, JENNY

Humans, they are a mixed bag! They come from all ends of the spectrum from good to bad. Makes it kind of confusing sometimes. I am still waiting to see what goes on in this place. You can be in a good space but then have 'elements' that makes me want to go away as far as possible. The jury's still out for me.

–CW

ALL SEEING EYES, BURRO, GELDING

To really be able to see is of such wealth! When you can see others' inner glow you can do or say something that will help it shine out. So we can help this world that needs our help. The more we practice seeing the more we learn how to see. You just have to practice every day. I do. We can help our world. I think it must be our turn to help because we're here now. I hope you will learn to see.

–JG

ALLEGRO, BURRO, JACK

First of all, let me share with you that we are pleased that this sharing is continuing. We wish to help our human brothers and sisters along their journey, if they choose to let us. We have always been there for our human relatives, and many times no one has been aware of this.

It is good that some are ready to reconnect with the rest of creation. And how wonderful that we can communicate with each other. We of the animals world (yes, you too are animals), so let me clarify that I mean the non-human animal world, have always communicated this way. So did you in the distant past, and most of you as young children. We wonder why your adults tell you that this is not possible, and then you believe them, instead of believing what you know in your hearts.

Many things that seem to divide us would not divide us if we all spoke and listened to each other. And if we all listened with our hearts.

Think of that... all listening in love with our hearts. To each other in respect and kindness. Would that change this world? You decide for you. I believe it would. Thank you

–W

ALMA, HORSE, MARE

I've been waiting for this!

You are all leaders on the earth. I know about leadership, and I have things to learn about leadership. So do you.

Soft leaders aren't effective, so we all get afraid of being soft. I get soft sometimes. Hard leaders get other problems, like scared, weak subjects, or rebellions. And subjects without any ideas of their own. I get hard sometimes.

Seems to me that there could be something that is better. What about creating a whole different kind of leader? Let's see. Maybe someone who just is a certain way, and gets respect. And then everyone follows unless they have a better idea. Then the leader listens because the leader is that way.

That's the way it is now, anyway. We are leaders and we are a certain way, and everyone follows us that way. We have to be careful then, how we are. We have to be real careful about what our certain way is. That's so we know what we are creating behind us. We might create what we don't want.

You know, that means we better know what we are doing. What a concept!

You are more powerful than you think. You don't have to be afraid of being unimportant. You will get more important and even more followers if you are a certain way of kindness and gentleness and understanding and giving the benefit to each being that they are good. You don't have to make shows of power. That keeps you from knowing how powerful you really are. So be it.

Good luck!

–JR

ALYSSUM, DOG, FEMALE

If they (humans) could only bound about in the joy that is deep in their stomach we might all get along so well.

I guess they can't. They have fear of us. We have fear of them. We might hurt each other.

Seems so shameful since we really love each other so much.

Well, let's do other things with that love. Let's find joy in other ways.

We have a quietness in joy too except we can't always be quiet about it. We have to let you know we are excited about joy and mostly we don't care if you know because we just feel so good about feeling so good.

We can have quiet happiness too. It's easier for you to have the quietness. That's a new kind of joy. Just the warm part. That's when I put my chin on your foot. For the warm part. And I give you the warm part too.

Hands and feet do that. You touch me with your hand. I touch your foot with my chin. Oh, O.K., chins do it too.

So we can get to the joy in your deepest part of your stomach together. Maybe just by being warm together.

The most important thing is being warm together. We need to find a way to do that. That is very, very big. So all of you and all of us can be taken into the warmth.

But you know we have to make the warmth, and then I think there is always enough room for everyone. And everyone can bring warmness too. So then the warmness gets bigger and bigger and bigger. Who knows? It might take over the world.

–JR

AMELIA, MULE, FEMALE

Well, thank you for this opportunity. It is well within my desire to see humanity glow and grow. And prosper. We all should prosper. Prosper in our minds and hearts and within our physical beings. We all should have that opportunity.

Bless those humans who are ready to open, ready to blast off from where they once stood. Bless those humans who are ready to be fully open to the possibilities that await them. We await them, us animals. We have waited for millennia. We have been very patient and we do it with love. In love, there is no timing, no time. In love, there is just being. Bless those humans who are being now. Bless them, for in their being-ness, they can see us. They can witness who we really are. They can witness their own gifts. It is as if a light switches on for them. It is as if they have never seen before, those blessed humans who are awakening. It is our desire and gift to greet and meet you now. We have always been willing. You, up until now, have not been able. Now it appears as if the time has come when you are ready, willing and able.

We greet you blessed humans. See yourselves. Aren't you glorious? See us. Are we not glorious? Yes, you who see can see us, you who see can have the glorious perspective that we have always had. Thank you humans.

Thank you for awakening. We have waited. We have watched. Now you are ready. Thank you for all your hard work. Thank you for getting here.

–JR

AMIGO MIGUEL, BURRO, JACK

Look for the beauty around you so you don't miss it from greed or fear or both. You know, I think they go together.

So find joy in the moments of shining light, even light that comes at dawn and light that fills the heavens during a sunny day, and the light of lightning and the light that fills the sky as the sun sets. And the light from the moon as it shines and reflects our magnificent countenance; our magnificent Mother Earth countenance.

Be learning that the light of heaven reflects on us, and reflects us. It reflects our light. We have light, too. That light gets buried behind fear. Then fear becomes something ugly that hurts everyone, especially the one who has that fear.

Everyone knows of fear. Everyone has experienced fear. Everyone operates from fear. Everyone is directed from fear.

Oh, to be free of that controlling element! It is too controlling. Controls us completely. Could we all get together and sing a chorus of love to the fear? So the fear can melt into its own glorious loving beauty of Self.

Does that make sense to you?

Perhaps not.

Please let it sink into your heart and change your fear into your freedom of love. And love. And love. And always love.

I have made that change. It is possible for all.

Do not wait. Do it now. Let your light burst out into joy and freedom.

I send you my freedom and my love and my light.

–JR

Burro, photo by Deb Derr

AMOURE, BURRO, JENNY

I have been expecting you! I have come from a beautiful place and bring news of hope. There is a wondrous change taking place for our planet. Mother Earth has begun a healing process in her very core. She is working from the inside out, as we all should. And she is in need of our help!

Humans can aid this process by disassembling the old walls that have separated us for eons. These are barriers that separate not only humans, but humans and all species. Be aware, this is a difficult and monumental task. These walls constructed of stone and mortar has had many years to bond and settle. At first it will feel like an insurmountable task. You will feel as though you are chipping away at a great structure and will feel compelled to give up. Don't give up! For the sake of Mother Earth and all her inhabitants, do not.

Once the old walls are gone, we can at last feel the true universal connection that binds us all together. This connection is of divine design, and much stronger than anything made of brick and mortar. This natural connection encircles humans, animals, elements, all beings. When this is re-established, you will be floating! You will wonder why you existed in the former state of separation for so long. This is where true change and healing can expand at the speed of light.

If you are unsure of what steps to take first, prick up your ears... pretend you have those of a burro! Listen, tune in, ask. Ask and you will hear your own directives.

I am excited to bring this message of hope and goodwill to you. As you go down this path, know that you have many by your side. I will be walking beside you and can carry any load that you cannot bear. This will bring us a wonderful shift in consciousness and in being. Trust in that, and take the small steps that you can today. For we must all play a part if our earth is to heal. With your diligence and chaste purpose, we will see amazing results.

Bless you; we are all children of the universe!

Please go out and spread the word.

–CR

ANGEL, BURRO, JENNY

I am so happy I am home, my forever home. I was here before, and here I am again. How many humans have a forever home? Are you living at your real home? Are you living where your heart and soul belong? I hope so! And are you living in and with unconditional love?

I am, and I hope you are. I let my human pick my name, and I love it. Who wouldn't? Let love be your guide to all you do. Love your friends, and love those who would not be your friends. Doesn't mean you always like them, or even trust them. You should follow your heart and your intuition there as well. But still love them. After all, we are all one.

–W

ANGELINA, HORSE, MARE

Don't be silly. You are all so silly. I hope you find the silliness in all that worry that makes some of you so sad and some of you so depressed and some of you too frightened to be in life and that makes some of you mean. I had meanness in my life and it wasn't just silly. It makes big scars in the heart. That's what happened to me. But it's silly to be serious about silliness. All those worries just pile up and don't help anything. They hurt everything. So, if you want to get rid of your worries and sadness and your depression and even your anger, go away from the silliness.

Silliness is crowded and alone at the same time. Silliness has too many who buy it and also keeps everyone from loving each other and being close. It makes a big yucky pink wall around the silliness and doesn't let anyone else in. So everyone has to be alone with their silliness even though everyone is silly.

If you graze for a day, you will feel much better. If you roll everyday at least one time you will be stronger and happier. If you gallop through fields at least one time a day, you will feel free. If you whinny at your neighbor, she will be so happy and might even whinny back.

Breathing on each other makes love permeate to the core of our being and then there's no room for silliness. Nibbling and chasing is friendly and then each time you nibble and chase someone, you will have a new friend and both of you will be out of the silliness. Eat your carrots. Eat your oats. Chew your hay really well. Don't swallow too fast, it gets stuck. Keep your stall clean and fresh so it always smells good. Don't let yourself get dizzy. Smell everyone's waste water so you know them well and then you know who's visiting you and you can feel good for being visited and safe. Never mind, you know all that. I'm just telling you so you don't forget.

–JR

ANNA, BURRO, JENNY

I don't think so.

I don't think of humans except for Barb & Wynne.

Maybe it would be good if I thought of humans.

They're very curious.

You are so eager. Maybe ease could help you feel like you are more a part of everything. You want to be a part of everything and can't, so you ignore and reject the life of everything. That must make you lonely; if you see no life in everything. I think you see no life even where it is. So you must miss lots of life in you.

THAT must be lonely.

Well, I am giving myself ideas now. I want to look around and see the life in everything. It might be good for you to do the same. It's a way to not be lonely.

Have fun.

–JR

ANNA BELL, HORSE, MARE

Humans? My, why surely I could come up with something. Hmmm... let's see.

I would like to share the love I have for you. I would like for you to feel my love. Really feel my love. It is not something that you have to do anything with. It is a feeling. It is a palpable, nice, warm, fuzzy feeling. It is such a large and

Anna Bell with Raven, photo by Deb Derr

grand expression that I wonder how many humans could actually feel it. Really, truly feel it.

It is expansive, you know. It will expand you, if you feel my love. And you will get to know me, and I will get to know you. Come one day, here, and let's breathe together. Humans have a tendency to need some thing in order to feel. Love knows no distance. You could feel it right here and now if you care to, want to, and desire it. But if you can't, no worries. Come here and meet with me.

Come here and breathe with me. We would be friends then and we could do wondrous things with the love that we have together. Wondrous, marvelous things. It will expand you, you know. It will change your feelings about yourself and your world. It will change you. Come breathe with me if you would like a change.

–SM

ANNE MARIA, BURRO, JENNY

This book is the start of many consciousnesses coming together fulfilling a prophecy to realign and heal certain issues at hand. Hold true to yourself as we hold true to you. Heal yourself as we heal you. As we are all one. Become one with us. We are waiting… patiently.

–S

APRIL, BURRO, JENNY

I would love to share that we animals are humans too (smile)! We would like to have a good life and be with family. We would like to have good food and those that care for us to be kind. We would prefer to live with our own kind because we learn from each other. When you separate us from our families, we don't learn as quickly. Some things we don't learn at all. The elders share information and more than just every day things. They share the answers to the world when you are just with them. It vibrates out of their skin, out of their bones. Their bodies tell a story, and their souls vibrate to the truth. That is what I want to say. Please don't separate us from our families.
Tell them that there are good humans and some that haven't learned too much. I like both. Tell those that haven't learned too much to spend time with their elders. They will teach them much. Thank you.

–SM

ARAPAHOE, BURRO, JACK

I watched the two of you every day and you were the ones who were so incredibly beautiful!
I heard you use this word incredible so many times. I finally decided it meant 'you reach beyond'. I thought it was a marvelous word. I wondered in the beginning if that was someone's name. I guess you could say it is a good name. That is what I would name you.
You are my first human friends. I love you.

–JG

ASHLEY, HORSE, MARE

I don't know if I have anything new or different to add to what others have said. My last body had physical problems. Sometimes humans looked at me with pity. That is uncomfortable. I did have, as my friends said, a less than perfect body, but they also knew I was a perfect being none-the-less.

Physical conditions are just that. I lived where several ones had physical conditions, yet all were accepted as they were. One named Kyro made it easier for my humans to see us without the physical conditions. He was different, but only physically. They came to see that physical differences are not important. Look to the spirit, the soul. That is the real being. At that level, there are no differences. Thank you for considering my view.

–W

AURIEL, BURRO, JENNY

You have received many messages.
We hope all can learn and listen to our words, our hearts.
Please give thanks to all things, to all beings
as we beings give thanks for you.
As you are also our heart.

–S

AUTUMN, BURRO, JENNY

Yes, thank you. Please let humans know that we are more than lumps of flesh and bone. We, animals and particularly those of the burro expression because I know them best, have much to offer you. Not in ways of doing for you. No, what we offer is more a way of being. We can teach you that. Being-ness.

If you could slow yourselves down, shift out of your minds, feel your own bodies... and now, that is another big thing to talk about (feeling your bodies)... you would begin to feel your own being-ness.

We do it all the time. That is how we live. And you know what that will do for you, dear humans? You will know your self. And your self is pretty marvelous. Just like us. To feel us is to know us, I like to say. To feel us is to love us. We feel you and love you.

Could you do the same for us?

-SM

BARBARO, BURRO, GELDING

That is a very good question. That is a verrrry good question. Thank you for asking. I would like to share, to participate. This is a good exercise. It is a very good idea. We animals have much to share with humans, with humanity.

Now, what I wish to say may startle some, but here goes... Humans, you are not the middle of a circle of life. There is no center. There is no one at this center. If there were a center, we would all be included within it. No... life on this earth can be more likened to a web. What one set of beings do upon this web affects the rest of the web, and those beings upon it, those beings upon it that depend on the earth to live. We all depend on this earth to live. You seeking to dominate your energies over other beings, seeking to do what your ego-drives seek to do, is killing this planet. Your egos are killing this planet.

Now, if you would like to settle into yourselves and seek the truth of who you really are inside, in your hearts, you would be able to see this. And be able to feel it. You who dominate the earth with your egos are mind-driven. Minds cannot create as the creator has created. Surely, you believe you have created many wondrous things. And I suppose on some levels you have. Surely you have.

You must come to recognize that your minds cannot create the magic of what the earth and all of its inhabitants have to offer. Surely you cannot believe that everything upon this earth is not here for a reason. A physical reason. A spiritual reason. A love reason.

Now, I mean you no harm by these words. I am in love with life. All life. I wish to touch your hearts with my words. I wish to awaken your hearts so that you may see as I see. See what it is that I see. You are all loving underneath. You are all loving in your hearts. The earth's heart strives to connect with your hearts. All beings upon this planet seek to connect with your hearts. If you listened to your hearts, you would see what I see.

And... you would see me,
Loving you.

−SM

BAXTER, BURRO, GELDING

We are all here on this earth for a purpose and it is very important to act with purpose in everything that we do. If I walk to my feed bucket, I do it with purpose. There is a connection for humans and animals with the earth, the sun and the moon that needs to be honored. We need to walk and act with purpose so that we can better understand our personal roles on this earth.

We affect everything with our actions. We are feeding the sun, earth and the moon with everything we do, at all times. Our intentions, our thoughts and our actions impact all. This includes the air that we breathe and the water that we drink. It is all cyclical, it all connects. This sustains life.

I see all. People don't think so sometimes. I'm reserved but I have a strong presence in this place. Sometimes people trip over me. They push me to the side in order to move around me. I won't move. It's a game for me. I enjoy seeing how far I can take it.

–AA

BEANY BABY, BURRO, JENNY

It is ok cause you have called me this.
My name matters not... only my soul.
Thank you for asking again.
See where the Moon has been.
It sheds light on all of light.
Embrace the light, we are there.
Where are you?
–S

BEAU, DOG, MALE

I'm happy here. Always somebody to play with and be with, food & water too. Lots of hurt out there, lots of sad feelings, but here is warm and always sunshine no matter if rain.

All spirits are meant to be together and love, but that's not the way it works many places. Spirits here are happy and sad, but when they leave to other side, sad is gone and peace once more. Humans could learn from spirits if only they'd open and really listen to us. Wind, rain, sunshine and even death are all part of a greater plan. Humans get so sad over death, but it's not sad, even though missing is sad, the other side is wonderful and light and warm and sunshine.

I'd like to say to humans: Open up and accept what's around, don't cry or be upset. Life and crossing over is just part of a journey and everybody will be together again. Just have patience – like me. I have patience, lots of patience. I also like to talk – a lot, but humans don't like me talking some times. But other animal spirits here do. We get along. Humans need to have patience and accept. That's all.

–LB

BEAUTY, BURRO, JENNY

I want to share a message of hope and of unity with you. We are the same. When someone is abused, whether it be human, animal or otherwise, we are all abused. When someone is loved and lifted up, so are we all. I have met both of these conditions in my life. I thought at one point in my life that all of the love and hope in my heart had shriveled up and died, but today, my heart overflows with love! It is possible for you too. Love does not die; it springs eternal. With one tiny spark, it renews itself effortlessly. Please know this is true. Those of you who feel hopeless, let me tell you there is hope. During difficult days, keep your eyes on tasks and continue down your path. You will meet injustice and cruelty, this is certain. Do your best to get through it and know there are better things in your future. I know this now, and want to share it with you!

I have just met amazing humans who have saved my life. I have also met humans who abused me and did not care if I lived or died. I implore you...look at us, really look into our eyes and see our souls. You will realize that we are all the same. When you abuse me, you abuse yourselves. The separation and hierarchy between species is an illusion. Please break the pattern so that we can live in harmony.

Know that we do not mind working for you, not in the least! We are strong of spirit and are hardworking, and in this role we serve best. But work with us in a loving a respectful way. If this is done, everything will operate smoothly, as it should. Whatever you do to me, you do to every living being.

For those who do not have hope in their hearts, do not give up! Happiness and contentment may have thus far eluded you, but continue your journey with the knowledge that the sole reason we were born is to express our love to one another. This is the way we can achieve bliss. If you feel beaten down, get up and keep going. Sing your song to the world, even if it seems no one wants to hear it. Treat everyone you meet with the same love and respect you deserve for yourself. It is worth it...believe me, I know!

Thank you Beauty, is there anything else you would like to share?

Truly enjoy the little things in life, like a good sugar cookie! That is all I have to share today, thank you.

–CB

BECKY, BURRO, JENNY

I would love to say something, thank you for asking. It is, that people are into people not aware of the big picture, our World the one you and I live on, the one that we had made an agreement to uphold, care for and nurture. I ask you this… what happens when we don't tend to our agreement with the universe?

–S

BELLE, PONY, MARE

Let me first say that I thank you. I thank you for sharing our world. I thank you for teaching me things. And I thank you for loving me.
I would also like to say that time doesn't mean what you think it means. Time doesn't mean anything, really. It is something that is made up. All within this world will pass away one day, and all within this world will return. See? It doesn't matter about time. What matters is what you are here to do. Think about it. What are you here to do?
Me, I'm here to give to my brothers and sisters. I am here to give to you. My heart, that is. It is my heart that I am here to give. I am here to give you the best of me. The real me. The only me. Because there is only one of me, or ever will be. So that makes me special. And that makes you special too. Because there is only one of you. Got it? That is what I want to say.
Oh… and that the time is now to give yourself away.

–SM

BILLY, BURRO, GELDING

How can I concentrate on healing the World
when you concentrate on destroying it?
Knock it off!
–S

28

BITZY, BURRO, JENNY

Yes, cherish those experiences;
cherish love, life and all things around you.
After all, you created it.

–S

Eeyore: Photo By Noel Breen

BLUE (JAMANJI), LLAMA, MALE

Blue (Jamanji), photo by Janice Goff

I have much to say to humans like yourself. The first thing to talk about is the sunrise and new wealth of knowledge it brings on the morning air. There are a great many things unknown to your people. Forgotten things.

Now let's get something straight, the purpose of our communication is not simply to ask me to speak to you humans. You all have questions that you have not found answers to in your everyday world. You have machines and yet these don't provide the answers you seek either. So you at last, turn to the animals. It's been a long time coming. We've had many of the answers to the universe within our minds for a long time, but you were too deaf to hear. Now you are ready. It is good.

I ask that you sit comfortably with my ideas and broaden the landscape of your mind. What I may tell you may be hard to hear at first, and yet it's what you've been seeking in your hearts a long while now.

There lies on the horizon a vast universe. Much like that of your own. You can't see it with the naked eye, and yet it is there just the same. It's a place we all go to when you say we "die" though that phrase is erroneously used. It's much more of a rebirth, actually. A beginning that's been repeated time and time again. Over there are your answers. We animals embody some of them, though not all.

The meaning of life as I see it, despite its ups and downs and occasional crashing into the dirt, it about discovery and growth. And a unison. A place of living amongst and within. There comes a time in one's life when the outside that you see is no longer that which you really seek. What you really seek is Home. A place native to all of us.

Home is not that far away and you don't have to be over the horizon to experience it. Look around and know you are part of it. You are existing as one with it right now. There is no getting TO it. Or jumping a bridge in getting there. It's not a place. It's a state of being. You find it most readily when you sleep. But you find it at other times too.

Animals have known this a long time. Many of your kind run about looking for your mothers to provide it, or for it to appear in your physical homes. But it's not there. Not in the way you would like.

Do you understand what I say?

People need to quit looking outside themselves to find what they really want. Live in the experiences of life, breathe in the air and notice what is almost intangible. Emotions play a role here in guiding you to the next extreme. To the universe you really seek. Live in it. It will come to you and you will then exist like the animals. Serene and peaceful and living in the moment of every day.

To us there is little outside the moment. It doesn't do us justice to let go of the present to inspect what was or what is to come, because we lose focus of what really matters now.

And time is precious as you humans say. It is to us animals too. To all spirit. Remember this and know thyself. And you will be like us and the world will open to you like a flower in bloom, singing sweet songs in your ears. And you will really be existing in a way not tangible as before. You will really experience IT. The All That Is that dwells within you. Your own divinity.

How else can I put this? You have within you a wellspring of who you are that has eluded you for years. Many a few human barely touches the very edge of your own creation because you choose to focus on outside events vs. what is real.

One's focus should be chosen. Don't haphazardly look around or your senses will be overwhelmed and in order to control yourselves you will have to mask your real feelings of experience overload. The 'take in' should be a conscious choice. Make a wise decision and go with that. You have heard me well. This is my message.

Danielle: *Is there anything else you'd like to share?*

There will come a time when the planet ceases to be part of creation. When all things know who they are and we stop playing the guessing-game. When this happens, life will settle and you will graze upon the earth like us in earnest and with great respect at having found your divine inner being.

Danielle: *Blue, I don't understand the phrase "when the planet ceases to be a part of creation." Please explain.*

I mean so only in the physical manner. All matter of life rejuvenates and is reborn into life. But not always will there be this chaos of life that now inhabits your species. We will evolve forward together out into dimensions and awareness outside your current mode of thinking. When the lines adjust to this frequency, new life will flourish and it will be like a rebirth of a planet from the old. It will be like new. The old ways will be released out of need and turmoil and life will be different.

As high as you count the stars in space, that is the distance we must travel to reach a newly created earth. We have a ways to go yet, but we're half way on our journey. It will be done.

–DT

BLUE GLORY, BURRO, GELDING

What is everyone else talking about?

Janice: *I am just doing the writing, not asking questions. They are talking about love, life where you are now, life with Wynne and Barb, some of their memories, stuff like that. Do you have anything you would like to say?*

Tell me what everybody else said.

Janice: *O.K., I'll read all the communication of the evening.*

Can we say things that somebody else has said?

Janice: *You feel free to say anything you want to.*

I love my long legs. I love my birth carrier. I love to run. I am welcome. I am loved. I am wonderful. I still can hear. I still can smell. I still visit everyone. See how big I am! I didn't mind being talked to in a tiny voice. I really liked it running around and around everyone. Thank you for letting me be born where I could see you. Little bodies are so much fun! I am a teacher. I am a great leader. I think that's all. I liked what everyone else said.

–JG

BOB, BURRO, GELDING

Soak your soul on the river of your heart, there is where,
the follow of your soul to your physical body will renew itself.
All else will flow and heal.
Have patience with this.

–S

BRANDY LOU, HORSE, MARE

Oh, yes. I'd like my human relatives to consider the needs of all other beings when they make decisions about land use. Surely there is enough for all. But that means that the needs of all are equal.

My wild relatives, the horses and burros who prefer living as free wild animals are being removed and forced to live as domestic animals. I was raised as a domestic animal, so I don't mind, but my wild relatives would prefer to have the choice. Of course, they adapt, but isn't there enough room for all to live as they wish?

Please remember to consider all when you decide. Otherwise, conflict arises, and that doesn't help anyone. I thank you for listening.

–W

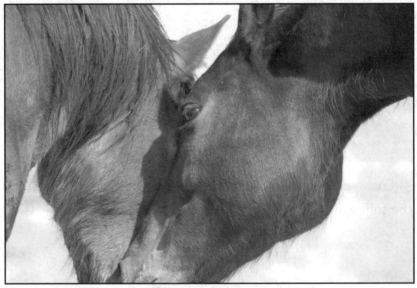

Photo by Deb Derr

BRAVEHEART, HORSE, GELDING

Thank you for asking me. I had pretty much given up on this lifetime. I was still angry from being torn away from my birth mother so young. We had agreed to do this, and then someone else decided that didn't matter. When I objected the only way I could, I was severely beaten. Why or why, I wondered, couldn't humans listen to us, and understand. Don't they know we have feelings, wants, and desires? What happened to make them so?

Well, I've learned that some do! That gives me much hope. All of us here are grateful to be heard, and talked WITH, not to. And I know from listening to my human relatives here that other humans are reconnecting with the gift of communication. Just think... if we can truly communicate with each other, the possibilities of peace and understanding that will exist. We understand that humans in general have lots of other things to re-learn, and all of that will be easier, we think, with communication.

The Great Creator created us all, not just humans, and we know the Creative Force didn't make junk.

I truly am fortunate to be here. I've got a large family now, ones that care, and love unconditionally, and respect.

I'm still learning, or so I hear, some lessons that I might have learned much younger, about manners and getting along. Well, I have those who will and are teaching me.

Once again, humans might become more aware that all of the earth's young learn from their family especially their moms if allowed that time. Not just human children, all children.

So come see us, and observe us, and feel our love and friendship. Let's all be friends now that I've learned trust again.

–W

BUTTERSCOTCH, CAT, MALE

It is best to move through the world with grace as well as you can. If you don't have grace in your body, you can have it in your heart and mind. You can make grace happen even if your body doesn't know what grace is. Your spirit always knows. And you just have to listen to your spirit and give your spirit a very strong voice to sing grace with the most graceful meow. Then your body will feel grace as a blessing from all of life.

Grace is a blessing you know, from inside your heart and inside your spirit. And when you are generous with it, it comes back to you and is generous to you too.

It is best to be generous to those who need generosity even when they are not appealing. They might be angels in disguise because they might have angelic hearts... big, deep, spiritual, angelic hearts. Then you allow them to stay with their angelic piece, that strongness. That is what our angel pieces are, you know... strongness.

If you don't know your angel piece, pretend to be a graceful cat. Cat angels will help you to know your strong angel piece. You have no idea how happy and content you can be with that kind of assistance.

You may have to be a little humble. That's hard, even for cats. But we actually know how very well, and we can tell you. So trust us, please, and really listen so you can have an independent angel piece of your own that gets strong and shines all over you.

Bye!

–JR

CAMILLE, MULE, FEMALE

Well, now, let me get my thoughts together. This is special, and I'd like to share something meaningful with you.

I am one who didn't appreciate being ridden. Not all of us do. Some love it, and others don't. It would be wonderful if humans let us have some say in the matter. If you think about it, those who don't want to do it will not do as well as those who do.

Now there is a lesson for more than just riding. All of us have some things we are better at and really love. Wouldn't it be grand to let everyone do the things they like? I suppose that everything would still get done, and everyone would be happier.

It is wonderful when your people just let you be yourself. That's another one I suggest humans could learn from. Be yourself, not someone else. Let others be themselves, not who you want them to be.

Just some things to think about, please. And thanks for listening!

–W

CANTOR, BURRO, GELDING

I'm actually shy about this.

I know my actions weren't exactly what you'd call huggie, kissie, but it's because I am a deep thinker. I watch everything and everybody. It was very important for me to finally understand about the gentle being I was about. never quite understood all the human body languages, like the man who came with long fingers to cut off our feet (the farrier). But I think he had potential to have great ears like ours.

Actually, the human bodies were the most interesting. They could make their body tall all day if they wanted to. I realized it was because they didn't have the privilege of our large heads and strong legs to balance them in a length position. They would have been able to move more fluid if they were built for a length position like ours.

And I didn't have time to figure out why they spent so much time picking up our waste. That is not something we would do. I did not see them wasting and picking it up. But I did see them picking up the contained wild dogs' waste. But I did not see them picking up the contained wild horses' waste.

I also saw they went into a sheltered area when they left us. It was like the sheltered area on our side. Where we lived before, there was a sheltered area in the side of a hill but we never went in there. I wondered if they tried to have for us a sheltered area like that so we would feel more at home seeing something we remembered.

I did like them very much. It was hard not breathing with my birth parent anymore. But I very much enjoyed everyone there.

–JG

THE FIFTEEN + FERAL CATS

Sue: *(Feeling of big smile).*

Yes of course. It is a great honor to be a part of this. It is a great honor to live and to have lived at this place. It is a great wonder how so many of us (animals) can get along. We are many. We are many who have come to this place to learn and love and teach. It is within our spirits' paths to do this. To love, to learn and to teach. It uplifts us. It grows us. It grows you.

Sue: *Thank you. What are you here to learn?*

Ahhhh... much is learned day by day. Some of us have growing to do. Some have come from places not so rich in kindness and it has wounded us, wounded our hearts. Some of us know more, so we teach the others about letting it go so it doesn't stay in our bodies to hurt us any longer.

Sue: *What are you here to teach?*

We teach about stillness. We teach about giving to others so that the whole may survive. We teach about one for the many and many for the one. We teach about what it takes to grow in self-hood and then sharing that self with others. We teach about our catness, our feline madness (smile). We teach that to love is to grow. That is all.

–SM

CERRA, BURRO, JENNY

I am so puzzled about how you all (people) think, and I am curious and interested in that. Maybe I will learn that from here where I am safe and loved.

We just want that, you know, and we always have that. Our ancestors ran free in the same form and in different forms, many centuries back. And the love was our own love and that around us from a greater place of love. It only became that greater place of love because it was filled with the love of beings who ran free and who just loved life and the All of our world, the All of that breathtaking life around us-- the grass and trees and water and sky-- that put together equal the Shaded One of Sunshine, Earth and Sky.

The Shaded One is the spirit of the All and we gave It life as It gives us life. It did then and It does now. It does that even for you and all other kinds of beings, even when we think differently.

But you know, we all have to feed It. We all have to put love into the All to keep It vital and loving. I am willing. Are you?

–JR

CHAD, HORSE, GELDING

Enjoy each and every moment you have on this earth. You never know if it will be your last and each moment is precious. We go through life not enjoying each moment, thinking that there will be a million more of them. But there might not be and each and every moment you do have, live that moment to the fullest. Do not live in anger, frustration, depression, the lower frequencies. Look to the sky. Look to nature and see the beauty. See the peace. See the happiness and let go of all the negativity. Breathe in the positive.

Life can be so joyful, even when we are in pain. Just bring in the joy. Think joy and you act joyously. If you act joyously, another might see you and they will pause and look to the sky as well. They will also take in the beauty and their day will lift to a new height of happiness too. For that person's last earthly breath might be soon and isn't it great knowing that you passed on joy to another??

We are so grateful for the opportunity to be listened too. We are so glad that more humans are willing and able to listen, for their ears and hearts have been closed for a long time.

Thank you. Just breathe. Take a nice deep breath right now and release all of the negativity. Your day will be so much nicer And who knows how many others' day you can help to improve as well.

Have a great day. Many of them. Spread the joy!

That is my message to humans.

–MM

CHARLA, BURRO, JENNY

There are many things humans could learn by watching us and seeing how we live with each other. They, humans, desire to conquer one another. Not these humans living here, but many, many humans on this earth. Those whose desire is to conquer will be conquered. Those, whose desire is to feel love and care for others, will feel love and care themselves. Those who feel the desire to share fear and destroy will also be feared and destroyed. It is a circle -- it is a cycle.

Life is one of give and take and those, whose desire is to give, will receive. Mark my words, oh little one. This is the way of the world and the way of life. Humans should care for the earth and its inhabitants of which we all are. None are better than another. We are all one and desire for this feeling of oneness to spread across the world and into human hearts.

This is a difficult concept for humans to relate to. They do not see that what they are doing is destroying themselves. We are part of that web and that circle of life and we desire for the earth to be treated kindly and with respect. This is what we do -- we assist in raising the level of consciousness to the heights of how we live our lives. We are desirous of love and equanimity across the planet. This is what we desire to see achieved, and we are assisting in this process. How can one love when the heart is closed? How can one feel kindness towards all, if one does not treat oneself with kindness?

The circle of life is a give and take, up and down, open and out. Please tell them that. They are destroying us, our kind, the planet and all inhabitants with greed and using the earth in ways she is not desirous of being treated. This will stop and will not be allowed to continue. This is ordained.

Please tell them to tread lightly and kiss the earth as she kisses you. I am hungry now and desire to eat my meal. We are love all of us and we are one.

Good day.

–SM

CHARLTON, BURRO, GELDING

Yes of course. Thank you for asking. I have been waiting to say my peace.
I love to live! I truly love to live! How many of you can say the same thing? How many of you can say that aloud at the top of your voice speak, that you truly love to live? Say it... I love to live! Just try it. You can do it in private. We don't get much privacy around here, but then, we don't need it so much. Humans, I dare say, probably need more privacy. More time to spend all by yourself. So that you can feel if you truly love to live.

–SM

CHARLIE, BURRO, GELDING

Hmmm....I can tell you I'm kind of laid back; I like to watch the world go by. People need to be more like me. There's a lot of hurry in people, they don't need to be in so much of a hurry. It's better to walk slowly and think a lot, take time to smell and see. That's what's better. I like to eat – the sweet stuff tastes so good. I like to watch the others too. We don't always agree but we're family. I like this place and all the food and air and grass and sunshine.

–LT

CHEROKEE, BURRO, JACK

I used to be a younger, cocky guy. I only thought everything evolved around me. Growing up some, I found out rather quickly that I was part of an evolution. That I could control my change, so I spent time on this instead of controlling things and people around me. It's funny when you look back at who you were. It really does make me laugh. I don't take myself so seriously anymore though. Changing is much easier than it used to be because I don't rough myself up about things. It's much easier on my back, not carrying such heavy loads of stuff around. I have learned some rather nice things since being here and really enjoy everyone's company and singing.

–JG

CHEYENNE, BURRO, JACK

Glad you asked, I've changed my mind. I want to participate. Lots has changed here since that summer. Lots of learning, lots of good things. Lots of time to think and learn. I'm excited to be part of what we will all do here, or wherever we all move together next.

We can help things change for the better for all. That is very good. The energy here is incredible – there, I used your word, and it applies so well. I'm glad you know all who left their bodies are still here, either in body or in spirit. We've been with you for thousands of years, either in body or in spirit or in body.

We have a large group. To all humans, I suggest that you just go with it. Don't fight life so much. Learn and accept. It is an incredible journey, and much more so when you just let it happen. A famous member of our group once said "the love of possessions is a disease among them". Is that you he was talking about?

–W

CHRISTINA, BURRO, JENNY

Have you ever seen the sunset?
Have you ever seen the sunrise?
Nothing should matter between the two.
Leave your worries in the sun, not in your head
or your loved ones or your enemies.
Thank the Sun for its healing.
All is good.
–S

CHRISTOPHER BEAR, BURRO, GELDING

Well, I'm glad the subject came up. Some of you are aware of reincarnation. Others are not. We know it to be real. I'm one of many who have been here, this very place, before, and during our humans' present incarnation. If this offends you, I'm sorry. That isn't something I choose to happen. Just sharing my message and hope it reaches you. I'd hate to only be here once, for sure. And, when those humans you are with recognize you, that is really fun.

Someone else who lives here said it already. And it is true. When you feel the connection with someone you meet, that is why. The kind of connection depends on what happened before. If it was unpleasant, just let that part go. It's your choice to start clear this time. IF you want to.

–W

CHRISTOPHER R, BURRO, GELDING

I came from a different place. I was thin. I was tired. I was never given enough food. There was no hope. There was great despair. There were mean and greedy people that treated us badly. There was no respect and no honor. There was definitely no love in their hearts! I don't know how we were rescued but we were rescued and I was and I am so grateful!

Abuse and hatred has to be stopped!

All life needs to be honored!

Stop all waste like this!

I am tired - but please help!

Too much is wasted!

There are too many people who are destroying too much. They are not understanding. They are living in darkness, wearing out all others!

Please help others to be found and rescued. All life needs to be honored.

I am very tired but you can help!

Send LOVE - send ENERGY - help raise consciousness!

The bad guys who are greedy and abusing need as much help and love, if not more, than those being abused. We already know and understand love. We send and share love all the time. They do not. Man needs to learn how to accept and share Love, not block it out.

We are so happy to be able to share what is in our souls.

Listen carefully! All you should hear and feel is Love! Let it out of your heart!

Share deeply!

–RL

CHRYSANTHEMUM, DOG, FEMALE

I believe that you all must believe in yourselves in this crazy world.

I am a being of many colors. That means I started out one way thousands of years ago in wildness and now I am in a human family without all that wildness but still with some. And I have enough to make you think I am totally wild.

My wildness is a deep, important part of me, and I bet you have some too. We both need to honor it without being harmful. This is a dog struggle. This is also a human struggle.

Sometimes humans pretend they have no wildness and then they can't believe in themselves and then they have no integrity because they don't know who they are. That happens to us too but not very much because we know of those deep parts and we honor them, sometimes to human disappointment.

We are learning, too, about balance so we can believe in ourselves and honor all parts of us and then put spiritual boundaries around ourselves so our wildness can live and flourish without being excessive. That's a very tricky proposition. And as we learn it we know we are making history and paving the way for many others to make this a better world.

So I ask you to join us. I ask you to be with us so we can all be so close to ourselves and believe in ourselves.

And in each other.

–JR

CINNAMON, BURRO, JENNY

Slow down.

Munch.

Chew.

Swallow.

Be still.

Be wary only when your senses are keen,

and not from worry.

Be alert to change.

Change is good for you, so don't avoid it.

Love danger.

It's adventure, unless it's big danger.

Then don't be foolish.

Be around yourself long enough to get to know yourself

so you know what you really want, instead of

what you think you want to satisfy your taste buds.

Be serious. Not too serious.

Be silly. Not too silly.

Have humor all the time, even in sadness.

Be truthful with all pain.

Never let yourself go.

Never dismiss yourself.

Trust.

Especially yourself.

Life comes along then, and you can have it.

Amen.

–JR

CLAIRELLE, BURRO, JENNY

I would like to share myself with humans. I would like to share my heart. I am a heart-keeper and a heart-healer. So I share my heart with humans so that they will share their hearts with me. Feel me. Feel my open heart. Feel the beat of my heart. Feel the warmth of my flesh, my body, my heart. Breathe it in. Deep. Deeper.

Say my name, Clairelle. Now, what do you see? Do you see me? Do you feel my love? Do you feel the healing that is now going on in your body, in your heart, in your soul? Keep breathing. Keeping feeling me. I am here. I am not going anywhere. I am here to help you. I am here to help you heal your hearts. Stay with me. Stay with it. You can do it, you who are ready.

Now, come back another time. And another time after that. Call my name and I will be there for you. I love you dear humans. I share myself with you.

–SM

CLAUDIA, BURRO, JENNY

Don't treat us like packages. We're not beasts of burden to be shooed around. We are sentient beings, like yourself. We animals seem to have committed our lives to your work as humans and yet some humans seem less committed to our deeds in life.

The deeds of animals are many. We love the grass as we chew it. We cherish it with our every breath. Humans chew their grain and talk with their mouths full and don't seem to notice the nourishment between their teeth. This saddens me, for it is a part of them. As I am a part of you. The configuration of our lives is not like pen hash marks criss-crossing, but has a more even flow to it. It progresses nicely from its starting point, like a box stall, and goes forth out into the world, intersecting with the lives of others in a way that has truly great meaning behind it. It is just and clear and so pure in this fashion. Animals see the lines of life intersected and interconnected in this way. Only the humans don't and yet your lines cross with ours, all the same. Your ignorance doesn't make you exempt.

I speak now of love. How it brings us all together in this complexity of human fashion. Humans seem to think they have it sorted out, and yet they can't find a single lost hair in a haystack. It's because they don't look deep enough. They notice the surface matter vs. the essence of the being standing in front of them. I ask you to put on glasses and peer close. I have much to tell and the wisdom of years to share it. There is great tenderness in my eyes for you (humans) whom I liken to an unwedded one. You amble about without an attachment, seemingly lost from your creator. Alas, you are never lost, you just think you are. Or perhaps don't think you are.

Let me tell you a secret. Animals know your true nature not because we look at your head or even at your feet. We look at the surface energy that ripples out of you in a way you can't hide or control. It's a natural propulsion and it emanates into the air with a finest quality. Subtle. This is what we detect.

Why then do we (animals) not react to your every intent that may be of ill will or none at all? Because we are "we" being "we." "Me" being "me." In my place nothing stands before me that disassociates me from the creator of it all. I know you, we and him are connected like lines on a string or the spokes of a wheel. With this knowledge of connectedness, there is little to fear when you look at it from the larger view.

Some beings have the wider focus. This focus of which I speak- the focus of connection and of seeing the lines weaved together. Others have a narrow focus, namely the humans I have spent much time amongst. In no way do I term those with a narrow focus "bad". They just are living in a world with bigger eye blinders sitting on their eyes than most. Do you see?

I am complete in my words. Let us go on.

Is there anything else you'd like to share?

Thank you for taking in my baby and me. We are grateful for this calm environment and are graced by the presence of others of our kind. We are in a community. I feel like I am one of the lead mares in my quest to bring us out of the hills. To help lead this sanctuary to brighter days and bigger beginnings. I feel like I will be with you till the brighter scenery lightens the day.

Come to me in time of need and I will soothe. The planet is in turmoil, yet we peacekeepers have much to say in helping align those of you struggling within your places. Notice how still we stand. Do this and you shall stand still too.

–DT

CLOVER, MAMMOTH BURRO, JENNY

I want to share with you the meaning of life. Life can be wasted or lived. To truly live life you must be involved with the world and what's going on in it. This is important to each of us regardless of species. Those of us living simple lives in the desert are as capable of being involved in world affairs as decision-makers in the big cities. Involvement in life is more about awareness of details, the breath we take, whiffs of scent on the wind, the kindly word from a neighboring soul than decisions and actions that make headlines. Each one doing its bit will make a difference to the one and the whole.

Motherhood and fatherhood, if your species practices it, are not to be taken lightly. It is through guidance and nurture that the young learn to participate in life and become responsible leaders, teachers and parents in their own right. If you are chosen for this role, it is the most important you will be called on to perform.

One thing you can say about burros is we're good at holding to the course and, in doing so, we are good examples for mankind. Peace. Namaste, gentle friends.

–JGIL

CLYDE, MINI BURRO, JACK

People need to relax. They get stressed out over little things. If the thing won't matter to you tomorrow, don't worry about it.

People should be happy and free. Be happy. Spread joy. When you're happy, you'll make others happy too.

–TC

COCHISE, BURRO, JACK

Not everyone gets to see into our eyes.
                    –W

The Herd: Photo By Noel Breen

CORAZON DEL MUNDO, BURRO, JENNY

Interesting that I got my chance right after Mi Amito. Interesting, because my momma and I have been mother and child for eons. Sometimes I'm the momma, other times she is the momma. We sure like it.

I hope you are not surprised that this happens. I think you knew, just didn't know you knew. Would it surprise you to learn that you know everything? You do. We all do. It seems to be harder for humans do know and accept this. I'm not sure why, but it sure seems as if that's so.

If you connect with your inner self, your heart, you can know anything. We try to help you do that, and you are the ones who must do that if it is to happen. And it will happen. When, I don't know. It will, I know that. Hope it's soon.

–W

COREY, BURRO, GELDING

There is so much to say!

I didn't even know how big I had gotten.

Every time I've had this opportunity to look at myself, I saw how much bigger I've gotten each time. We don't really start out in the beginning as a little being... but when we're released to be a "one" and we see how big the Great Oneness is, some of us see small first instead of we're still Great Oneness first. I guess that gets us started thinking we're smaller than we are.

Anyway, I no longer think I am small. My eyes and mind have come together. I wish I hadn't spent so much time thinking about my smallness. I see how it made people I love feel so sad and helpless. I hope you won't think about your smallness. Because it just isn't true.

I haven't decided to come back yet. I don't really think there's any need. I love it here and there's so many who want to come back there to do better with everything.

I still love to watch the birds fly.

–JG

CRICKET, BURRO, JENNY

A Poem for Peoples
crickety rickety cricket
persnickety crickety too
rickety rackety roo
creakety wrobblety cricket
snuckery snickery doo
pickerty puckety poo
crickety rickety crickety

They can make my words mean whatever they want. The really smart peoples will know that it's not the words, but what you feel when you say them out loud that makes them mean things. Think about it!

–CM

CUERVO, BURRO, JACK

The human effort to capture and harness the spirit of life is as old as life itself. It's been done to build families and kingdoms. Sometimes it's been done to initiate a new change, an evolution of some sort. Sometimes it was done to add to the ceremonial traditions for greater affect. It hasn't all been done to create hurt and devastation.

Being responsible for what you capture is the important thing, especially when it's other hearts. The intent. Always the intent needs to be checked and re-checked. Maybe human effort will evolve itself to where it is so secure with its individual creation that it never has to capture again.

–JG

DAISY, BURRO, JENNY

Hi I'm Daisy and I just want to say that I love Mother Earth. I love my Family. Here at the Sanctuary we are all family, I like that!

Maybe that's what you people should do, be family with everyone. I think you could be as happy as me if you were like that.

–S

Refreshments with Friends, photo by Deb Derr

DAKOTA, BURRO, GELDING

I have an inner understanding of my place in the Universe. I know that my place is unique and the Divine has not incarnated in anyone else in just the same way that It has in me.
I am unique and forever individualized. When I really came to realize all this I knew I would never have to imitate anyone else or even long for things that others have. All good things and the good life is now manifest in my experience. I do not have to compete with anyone for anything. I am forever myself now. I am united with all selves, but always an individual and a unique self that I am.

–JG

DAN, BURRO, GELDING

When all is said and done,
we have lived,
we have breathed,
we have cried...
–S

Oneness and Friend: Photo by Lecia Breen

DAPPER DAN, BURRO, JACK

Look back at where you were and where you are now. Isn't it amazing? Did you realize that you were moving? All move at their own speed, and each determines what that speed is. It isn't a race, although often it's fun to move faster when you know you are moving.

You can stop and enjoy life at the same time you're moving on life's journey. I'm not talking about just running here or there, or getting more and more faster. I'm talking about moving forward on spiritual growth. In the end, I believe that is all that matters.

And the way you move forward is by love. Accepting unconditional love. It's everywhere, you know, if you are open to it. From the ALL, from spirits, trees, rocks, all living things. From us. It's there for you.

–W

DAY DREAMER, BURRO, JENNY

Yes, thank you. I believe that humans can do miracles. I believe that once humans decide what it is they truly want and what it is that is truly aligned with their souls, they can do miracles. Miracles are easy, really. They are very easy to come into being if you are in your being. That's a good way to say it.

Yes, miracles are easy to come into being when you are in your being.

–SM

DIAMOND, HORSE, GELDING

Surely, I have some things to share with humanity. I would enjoy it, yes, to share. Thank you.

First, I wish humanity to know that we "animals" are living, breathing, loving, feeling beings. We are not automatons, not machines, not unthinking and robotic beings. We have all the senses of each of you. We feel love, we think about our lives, we have preferences, we have dislikes, we have knowledge from experience, and we have foibles, as do you.

That being said (and it needed to be said), I would like to welcome you to this world, this planet, this earth. I would like to welcome you to share it with each and every species. I would like to welcome you to enjoy your stay, but do not wreck it for others. I would like to welcome you to find peace within yourselves, for when you feel peace, you treat each other of your kind, and kinds like us, with better and sweeter kindness.

We are all in this together. We are all on this same place, same time, same travelers, right now. I would welcome you to rejoice in yourselves because you have made it far. Now is the time to "be". When you feel the most sacred part of yourselves, when you no longer look outside of yourselves to feel good, then you will have peace. And peace you will share with all.

That is what I would like to share, and welcome humanity with. It is something I have thought about for millennium. It is important to impart, and important for me to share. It is my heart-speak. I share it with peace.

–SM

DOLLY, BURRO, JENNY

I have come to share love on the wings of an angel
I will come in and fill you with such joy and happiness and love-
   be all that you are all that is in your soul - be love
Give happiness to others
Let it flow through you - right into the hearts of others.
I came to be in a happier place - stop violence and hurting
   - blind it by the light
Stopping greed and hatred and violence
   by these means creates more love – show love! - open hearts!
Everyone is part of God so we are all one being - be Love yourself.
   and you are love to others.
I came to show others there are good people doing good things
   – the more good that is done out of Love - the truer it is
   Have Heartwings.   –RL

DOMINO, HORSE, GELDING

Oh Glorious Day! Keep your spirits high. Kick in the air. Feeling
carefree. Glad I'm here!   –BG

Autumn: Photo By Noel Breen

DOROTHY MAE, BURRO, JENNY

I want to talk to people about seeing beauty. I am lucky to have the time to spend my days seeing beauty. I have a song that I sing to myself that I want to share with people. Here is my song:

Early morning sun
Ground shadows on
Seeing beauty
Seeing beauty

Many legs moving (spider)
Fuzzy ears (burro)
Seeing beauty
Seeing beauty

Eating food munchy
Whinny-neigh-arumph
Hearing beauty
Hearing beauty

Wind sweeping earth
Shhh-weee-oooo
Earth mumbles grumble
Hearing beauty
Hearing beauty

Sun sits warm back
Hard ground feet on
Feeling beauty
Feeling beauty

Cool night air
Shhh-weee-oooo
Prickly in my nose dusty
Feeling beauty
Feeling beauty

Eyes close sleepy
Eyes close sleepy
Shhh-weee-oooo

–CM

DUSTY, HORSE, GELDING

Tell the humans that they are love. They have forgotten this over the years. It is time to open their hearts and eyes to this love. It is happening. It is here. Just like the loving people at Hacienda de los Milagros have done. They have found the need to fulfill love. Love of life - love of the animals.

Humans have evolved. They are growing in their knowledge and understanding. They will keep growing and learning at a much faster pace now. Love is in the air. Hot as it is sometimes.

I would like to share my love with humans, as all animals do. We are here to help you along this path. This is why we are all here - to live, learn, and grow in love. Pass this love along. Show this love to one another and they in turn will show love to another and so on and so forth. Grow in love.

Life is all about growing in love. It doesn't matter what life brings you, it is all about love and loving one another. We are all one.

I would like to share my gratitude for all the wonderful, caring people at Hacienda. This is exactly what I am talking about. LOVE. They show that love here.

Thank you.

–MM

EARTHA, BURRO, JENNY

I am about Mother Earth. I stand where she stands and feel what she feels. The moon approaches and she cannot feel the grace. She yearns for you people to awake in her glorious light and healing, but you are so unaware. Why?

What more can she do for you to acknowledge her? She gives you love, land, nourishment, minerals, precious water, beauty! What do you give her? Do you think of her? I only ask that you try.

–S

EEYORE, BURRO, GELDING

What is important that I have to offer humans? I don't know that I have anything important to offer humans, even though I am important. Hmm, anything I have is important to offer humans. Maybe that's a lesson we can all learn. That whatever is offered by anyone is important, because everyone is important, no matter how insignificant they may be.

I will honor all my insignificances and I believe it would be good for humans to do the same with theirs. We might all get along better.

To be insignificant is not to be insignificant. Insignificant is as significant as anyone or anything else. That really means that no one is insignificant and everyone is significant. That's the same as me being important, even if what I say is not so earth shattering.

Does one have to shatter earth and make a big splash to be valuable and significant and important? Little splashes have life and spirit and zest and wishes just like big splashes. The little ones are quiet about it. They keep it to themselves and enjoy it inwardly and don't even know when someone else notices because they are so innocent about that.

Little splashes may never become big splashes, and they still give so very much pleasure. They are dainty and delicate and speak to gentle sensibilities. Big splashes have their place too. They need to be noticed and heard and even have very big things to say that are important in the big way. They all need to know of the balance of it.

Now, am I a big splash or a little splash? Maybe both. Maybe sometimes one and sometimes another. That's the fun of it. To be satisfied with either is to be satisfied with both, and never to be disappointed no matter which is there.

What kind of splash was that?!?!!??

–JR

EEYORE, BURRO, GELDING

The meaning of life
It takes a lifetime to know that one It takes having faith in yourself to figure that one out. It takes patience too and trust that answers come as you go along in life.

Take us for example. Some of us have been ripped away from our natural homes. Our choices were to leave or to die. That's a hard one to figure out meaning but it has some.

Some of us have been born into the strangest situations, where our persons are not very responsible. That's a hard one to figure out meaning but it has some. We get abused and neglected. Does that have meaning? Yes it does. Always meaning comes after the sad event, not before. Always after. So the sad event is not welcome, the meaning is. Most of the time beings are afraid to review the sad event. If they do they will find meaning in it; meaning that fits their own situation. So meaning in life is personal and unique and each of us must be open and willing to find our own.

Jeri: So, there really is no one big overall meaning to life?

The one great big overall meaning of life is us Those of us who live it. We are the meaning.

To seek such an answer outside of self becomes disappointing and wasteful. Each of us must look inside for that meaning and not worry whether we are right or wrong It is our meaning, our very own meaning and that is what makes us strong We don't have to go to everyone else's meaning Whoa! Whoa! Whoa! Would we get lost!

Tell all humans, please, to trust their own heart; to get really close to their own hearts so their hearts can be trustworthy and then to trust them.

Meaning will unfold in your own unique way Cherish it. It is your meaning. Allow it to become very meaningful.

Go on now and do your meaningful thing.

–JR

EEYORE JUNIOR, BURRO, GELDING

(Note: He told me he was with three lady burros and there were men in pick-up trucks rounding them up to catch them for slaughter.)

What a waste - a big waste of life! All that beautiful life - that these men have no honor for life at all. We are losing the natural way of life. The beautiful and gentle souls are being tromped on by greed for money- and stupidity and unawareness. The natural processes of life are being swallowed up. Please help all wild species. All natural habitats are lessening and in danger from fire and pollution, by man's greed and thoughtlessness. Do not let us be swallowed up and disappear! We have so much knowledge of life and love to share. More awareness needs to be opened! Protect this beautiful Earth! She has given water and shade and sun and food, all in a natural order of life and death.

Many humans have not honored this process! Why does one species believe they can control and take over and make choices for all the others? That is not so! Do anything you can do to stop these humans with black and greedy hearts! SEND LOVE. Every day, every minute. PRAY - SEND MORE LOVE - SEND LIGHT - Everyone on some level needs love. If you all send enough love, maybe understanding will awaken people who do not understand that hurting one being, hurts all beings. We are connected - we can all help each other!

Send love in all forms - let it rain down on all - alter everyone's consciousness on all levels. Do not judge if someone seems to "get it" or not - they all do on some level, and sending enough love and light - all the time - will help people wake up, hopefully in time. Acts of love and kindness outweigh all others!

We have great gratitude for being rescued so that we may continue on our life mission to raise awareness - helping others helps yourself. It creates a better physical place to live and breathe, it creates a community of spirit, a connection of souls to raise total awareness.

It is about learning - growth - loving - sharing – awareness, and of course, Love. Being as one spirit.

Thank you.

–RL

ELENA, BURRO, JENNY

I don't think I was very brave when I came here. I was somewhat afraid. It didn't take me long to know the nature of my fear was in my mind. In my mind I was not comfortable, but finally the comfort of my body got through to my mind. Now I have fearlessness over being here.
It takes time and effort to get over a fear. I just want to tell everyone that there isn't any one person who doesn't have a fear. Fear can break your heart though. I try to take care of my fears as soon as I can. I don't want my heart to be broken because of something I don't understand.

–JG

EMILY, BURRO, JENNY

I just want everyone to know that nothing is great and nothing is small to the Divine, so we should never wonder if what we are going to do will be hard or easy. The Great Divine knows no hard and no easy.

–JG

Burro Saying Hello: Photo By Noel Breen

EMMA, BURRO, JENNY

Do not hold yourselves above all else; false pride is unbecoming. And it is false, make no mistake. We all have an equal inheritance to the earth and, I'm sad to say, most are more thoughtful, kinder, to this life sustaining body. Well, that is incorrect, isn't it? All others are more in tune with the earth. We align ourselves with its rhythms and laws and, therefore, coexist with Mother Earth in peaceful harmony. It isn't difficult. Yet, if you choose not to honor the earth, please do not think more of yourself than of those who do.

The secret to contentment is to know who you are, have faith in your ability to achieve what you set out to do and do today's work today without concern or worry about tomorrow's work for you have tomorrow to give yourself to that work.

Peace will come. Take one day at a time and trust that the needs of tomorrow will come in time. Worry is a waste of time and time is a finite commodity. Pace yourself and know that you are adequate in what you do. What doesn't get done is not vital to the big picture.

–JGIL

ESTERLINA, HORSE, MARE

I love humans. I love, love, love them. They are a fairly interesting species. I watch them. I like to see them and play with their energies. Some swirl with bright colors and lots of love radiating from their bodies. Others, well... let's just say that they are in fear.

You know humans, there is no reason in the world why you should be in fear. And by fear I mean hiding from yourselves. Hiding who you really are. Hiding from your very own hearts. And by fear I mean being afraid of others. Afraid of their intent to reach out in love.

Many times I have seen a reaching out to another only to see the energy get braced against and pushed away. Everyone wants love so open your hearts to it okay? There is no reason to be in fear of love. Love is what makes the world go round. And love heals. It will heal your hearts if you let it in. Don't brace against it... let it fully into yourselves and the healing will begin.

This is what I see. This is what I like to watch. When I see love extended and accepted into another, it makes me breathe deeply into my lungs, and I know that another being on this planet has been healed.

–SM

67

FAIR WEATHER, BURRO, GELDING

Guess Morning Dew was reading my mind. Of course he was. We don't have secrets. Only humans do that. It is very hard to be a human, by the way. I know I'm not sure I'd choose that way again.

I came here by choice, as we all did. I came here to let go of some past life stuff with another burro who came here after I did. I knew she was coming here, too. And I also came here to see if I could support someone else here in letting go of past stuff. IT was wonderful... as soon as the connection was recognized, all the past stuff was immediately released in so far as this person and I are concerned. The easy part is done. The three of us have cleared it all away. In addition, I was an enemy to many here in a past life. Poof, that was gone, forgiven, forgotten, just like that.

You can let go merely by intention, you know. And it isn't always easy, and you can do it. Forgiving yourself is the hard part. Of letting go of past stuff, just please remember, it CAN be done.

–W

FAITH, HORSE, MARE

Have faith in one another and in God. Everyday live your life in faith. Faith that the sun will shine. Faith that you will have water. Faith that the night will come. Faith that someone is watching over you - taking care of you.

You are never alone. There are so many that care for each and every one of us. Even when things seem like they can get no worse, have faith that you are loved. You are never alone. You are looked after by angels. I have faith each and every day that I am being taken care of, watched over, comforted. Whatever I need I have faith that my needs will be met. These needs may not be filled in the way we think they should be met, but our greatest good will always be taken care of. Have faith in that.

The sun will shine. The day begins with a sense of renewal. Every day is a renewal of faith. If I only have this one message to give, it is this. Faith will get you thru the day - no matter what you are experiencing have faith that angels are there surrounding you, comforting you, faithfully being by your side.

Ask them to help you. Ask them to comfort you and always remember to give thanks. Thank the sun. Thank the day. Thank the angels. Thank the day of survival. Thank the opportunity to learn and grow. Your day is a day to grow.

Grow spiritually. Every day you can get closer to God. The Divine loves it when you have faith. Such delight the angels feel also when you have faith in them and acknowledge it.

Remember, live your day in faith and your life on earth will be one filled with growth. Every day we are given so many opportunities to grow spiritually. Have faith that you too can achieve this - very easily. Just thank the angels. Thank the day. Thank God. If you keep your thoughts on gratitude your day cannot get any better than that. You will be lifted to new heights. Your focus will be taken away from whatever troubles you have and your focus will be on faith and gratitude. Many blessings to you.

–MM

FANCY MOON, HORSE, MARE

My message to you today would be to listen to your heart and take action. If there is an injustice that you feel strongly or passionate about, do your best to take positive steps for change. It takes bravery to do this. But if you walk your life path with integrity, say things that need to be said and do things that need to be done, then your heart will be light and happy! You can cause a sea change and inspire others. Do not fear consequences of your actions as long as your heart tells you that they are righteous and true.

You need not be sharp or confrontational with your words or actions, not at all. Do everything with love. They key is to make sure that you are always connected with your heart and follow through with what it tells you. Love is always the solution and the greatest healer, it will not lead you astray.

People who knowingly do wrong, who mistreat others or our Mother Earth, depend on the silence and inaction of others. They perceive silence is an agreement with their practices, so they continue. All it takes is one peaceful voice, one peaceful act to make a difference.

People who follow their heart give us all a great gift: a positive change in our collective psyche. For example, the people who took me in my darkest state, who did not discount me as others had before, who opened up their home and hearts and gave me a new life.

These people are vibrant and alive, I know because I look into their eyes every day, and pure love and light is reflected back. They are this way because they are connected with their heart's purpose and have acted upon it. And look what they have created! A loving oasis, a preview of a blissful state that is possible for all.

Have you been to this place? If you are able, come and see what is possible. We are all equals here. You will feel the love and spirit of cooperation encircling you. When this kind of environment is created, everyone wants to give instead of take. Our hearts are so full that they overflow – and so we must give. In the act of giving we fulfill our greatest purpose. Come here if you can. You will be inspired to create your own space like this one, where everything is right with the world. I have so much love in my heart for you. I was given a new life at a time when I had nothing to offer in return. I will dedicate my life to spreading the word and keeping the love growing in this beautiful place.

–CB

FITZER, LLAMA, MALE

Well, brother, this has taken a while. No matter, now is a good time. What do I want to share with humans in general? I've gone over this many, many times. And I've listened to all the others messages.

Perhaps one thing to suggest is that all of us who have participated in this endeavor (the book) say a few things in many different ways. Matters not what kind of body we are connected with. We all want humans to wake up to the fact that we are one, and while in body, we must share the space and resources of Mother Earth. Of all the thousands of kinds of us that live here on this Earth, only ONE lives as if it is separate from nature. We see movement towards rejoining the real world on many, and further retreat and hardening in many, many others. Do they not know that this is a critical time for Mother Earth?

I say to humans in general that we hope you will rejoin the rest of us. You are part of the ONENESS, like it or not. And since you are part, why not start acting like it? Please stop being roadblocks to the healing that is started. If you don't stop, you may get run over by those who wake up. Mother WILL heal, with or without you. It is your choice. Please do!

–W

FLOWER, BURRO, JENNY

I'm here, I'm here! I've been waiting and waiting for someone to talk to me. I don't wanna be left out, I want my turn to talk.

Well, first of all, life is beautiful now…what you make it. It wasn't always beautiful for me, but it is now. I have plenty of food and people to be with, other spirits too. Life is like a rainbow, a beginning, a hill to climb, but once you're at the top and go down the other side, it gets a lot easier. We have feelings too, some humans don't realize that. They put us away, out of sight, and forget about us. That hurts!!! They don't see the beauty of our spirit or the other spirits around. Where I am now is good, people are kind. Humans need to really pay attention to us, stop and listen. Look into our eyes, listen to what we say. There's a whole other world that humans don't see, it's a beautiful place. Spirits are kind and playful. It's fun here, but it'll be funner on the other side. Humans will have fun too, on the other side, when it's their turn to cross over.

I like being here, even though I'd like humans to talk to me more and pay more attention to me. I'm comfortable here and I like my life here. A hug or two around my neck or pats would be good…I'd also like a long brush on my back. I hear food now so I have to go. Thank you for talking to me…it was fun.

–LT

FONTANA, HORSE, GELDING

Joy is in the hearts of all. Sometimes it is buried by worry, guilt, fear, pain, grief, want, sorrow, or loneliness, but its spark remains ready to be awakened by a treasured memory, a chance encounter, a friendly gesture, a kind word or a whiff of scent in the air. Don't give up on the possibility of reawakening the joy – for yourself or for others.

I share my love for the world and all that is in it. Be at peace in the knowledge that no one, no "thing," is unloved, for the truth is there is love saturating all things, appreciation spreading out over the world and its creatures from many of us. It is our role, some of us, to love, not deeply focused on the one, but widely focused on the whole.

The love I feel for you is personal, deeply focused, and abounds with appreciation. You have given me a chance, an opportunity to continue my work of loving all things and, in doing so, I we make the world a better, kinder place. Take heart that your efforts are worthy.

–JGIL

FRANCISCO, BURRO, GELDING

Whee… life is fun to see with eyes as all things
new bedew my eyes as all things new be-chime my ears
as all things new be-ruffle my hairs to be to see to hear
as if born now new at every chunket of time it is to be alive
at every splurgle of sun lights moon lights wind lights is to know
the hidden inside and be forever a wee one like Francisco who
is born recently new and live alive vibrantly for all the spans of being.

–CM

FRANCISCO, BURRO, JACK

Ask them (people) to please enter a cave (a horse trailer) or small area
with fences around it and stay there for a while. Ask them to do that
and understand our experience. To understand the big change this
really is for us. Tell them thank you for having the courage to do that,
because I think it will be hard for them to do that. It is hard for us.
We have much to get used to, and we do. We too have courage. Ask
them to hang from the sky without knowing what will happen. Tell
them that believing in their own hearts will help, because then it
doesn't matter if you live or die. Ask them to check to see if they truly
can believe in their own hearts. If they can't, they better not do it.

–JR

FRECKLES, HORSE, FILLY

Humans possess great gifts to share.
Everyone needs to share their talents and gifts with the world.
–RK

Lilly: Photo By Noel Breen

FRIEND, BURRO, JACK

Hello. We of the animal kingdom would like our friends of the human kingdom to recognize that we are all of the animal kingdom. We are not separate, nor are you.

Yes, we have some differences, but those are very minor in comparison with how we are the same. We are one. We realize that humans deal with some things that we don't, in particular what you call money. IT is only really of value depending on how you use it. Is it valued more than your soul? I hope not.

We must work together as equals to heal Mother Earth. We each have our parts. We wish all to be as connected to Mother Earth as we of non-human animals are. As are all the grasses, trees, rocks, and all that is. We are one. Please remember, we are one.

–W

GARDENIA, BURRO, JENNY

I haven't been treated very well in my life upon this planet -- this was a surprise to me -- that humans would treat others unkind.
Some say humans don't know love as well as others, but I don't find this to be true of all humans. This is a good thing, but I am wary of some people and do not wish to be in their presence. It is unfortunate as I have much love to share and much to give… it is their loss, I suppose. These people do not know what they are missing when they can't open their hearts enough to feel what we have to offer… what I have to offer.
I am Gardenia… a flower… a mere speck in this kingdom, but one who has many, many gifts. I send my love through the ethers. I share of myself with others; even those who don't wish to share theirs with me. I am a volunteer ambassador for my kingdom. I send love waves through

the ethers --this is one of my gifts. People receive it even if they are not aware of my presence. These people receive my love unexpectedly and sometimes it helps to unfreeze their hardened hearts. But somehow others will not receive and are stuck in their places of hardened hearts. They do not wish to be this way, but tell themselves they have no choice… this is what life has done to them. But this is not true. Life has not done anything to you.

Look at me, I have been mistreated in my life, but I still have much love to share. I find ways to share it in ways that I can. You are what you do to your own life. It is your choice how you receive and it is your choice how you take. This is truth upon this plane of existence. People have choice about whether their hearts are open enough; there is always room for more openness. This is what I do within my realm -- I assist in opening hearts. I am a heart opener! And I am good at it.

I will come into my own soon enough. I need time to gather myself up and take more training with those that are here, but I am a powerhouse of love, a love of respect and reverence for all beings… even those that maintain the closure of their hearts. They will one day change, but perhaps in the not too distance future. This is a shame, but they will change one day. I will help them. They must be desirous, and most are, but I will help them if they would just ask.

Treat me kindly and I will give you my love. Treat me badly, and I will give you my love. This is ordained in the nature of things. This is one of my gifts and my role upon this plane. I am love and I will share it. We are one. Good day.

–SM

GARTH, BURRO, JACK

I know about blessings. I have a few blessings and that is all I need. I am alive is number one. I am well taken care of is number two. I have love is number three. I have peace is number four. Maybe there are more. I don't know. Those are the most important. Oh, wait, number five is I have friends. Well, that kinda goes with love.

It seems to me it's very important to remember your blessings, and to think about them a lot, so you don't dwell on the problems. It's fun to think on blessings, because the more you think on them, the bigger they get. They even feel bigger. What, you say! Your imagination, you say. Maybe, I say, but I don't think so. Try it. You'll see.

I wonder if humans have few or lots of blessings. (To Wynne and Barb, you always tell us we are your blessings, and if we all are blessings, there are so many of us that you have many blessings. You could even share your blessings.)

It is a good idea, you know, to share your blessings. They multiply then. Yes, they do! Don't deny it. You just don't know how to count them when they multiply. You count them by feeling the joy in you grow and grow as you share them. That's how. When you have lots of blessings, it's a good idea to share them with someone who doesn't have a lot of blessings. Peace be with you.

–JR

GERONIMO, BURRO, JACK

My dream is to have my family live in a peaceful society, and help to create a reasonable society in all respects. I want to contribute to my community and larger society, and help reduce the destructive forces in the world. The only way to begin is learning how to relate to myself. Then I can expand from there.

What each of us needs to do depends on what the world presents to us. Keeping in mind we are co-creators in our world and society, but first within ourselves. That's why the names of warriors in different warriorship traditions are different. It's a unique and personal journey. I might be fully as brave as you are but I also might be a light hearted and humorous soul, where you might be serious and a deep thinker. Or a tender soul. Or an emotional one. This is all fine. Whoever we are; whatever we are called or call ourselves we must take down the barriers and open our senses. There are no rule books. You just have to tap into whatever energy you need to shake you up. Open your senses, rattle your soul, awaken you. Free yourself to experience and proclaim your truth. Claim your truth because the natural affect of who you are has constant affect on our world.

Thank you.

–JG

GLORIA, BURRO, JENNY

Well, what shall I share? Many of us are sharing a similar message, and this is for a reason. Maybe I can say it so it finds an audience in some easier than others, and if all of us share, more might listen and hear. There is, after all, only one basic message, and this is limitless unconditional love.

If you truly live in that knowledge, no problems or issues can affect you in a negative way. If you are not in that place yet, you might want to contemplate why. What in your present or past is blocking? We support your clearing, and only you can do it. We send you unconditional love. Can you feel it? It is all around you.

–W

GOLDEN ONE, BURRO, JENNY

I would like to tell you about miracles. Unlike what you might think, they are around us everywhere. I don't mean the miracle of life proceeding as it is meant to do. I speak of true miracles, of life restored where there was no hope, of hope restored where there was despair. I am surrounded by such miracles, yet I do not take them for granted. Each is precious and remarkable in its own right. Each creature is blessed and worthy to have been blessed by his own miracle. Look around you. If you need a miracle, know that it can occur. Disbelief is the destroyer of miracles – trust, and your miracle will bless you because every being is worthy of a miracle.

I share my love to all. I am not stingy in love. It is what I have in abundance and offer freely to every creature. I offer it because it is my goal in life to provide warmth and happiness for others.

I am happy, peaceful and content. You have given me my miracle, as you have given so many others. I choose to use my time in sending love to others, not as payment for a gift beyond measure, but because it is in my heart to send that blessing to brighten the world.

–JGIL

GRACE, HORSE, MARE

Oh, neat! I like to talk to humans. Sometimes I am shy of talking to humans. They are so powerful that I feel very, very small even though I am bigger.

I think size has nothing to do with power. I think heart has to do with power. I think good hearts have good power, and all hearts are good, so all hearts have good power.

Isn't that hopeful?

I guess power gets mixed up and sometimes someone doesn't know what it is at all. Then it's hard to use it. Or at least hard to use it right. I wonder why we have power? To survive? I suppose. I don't know why else to have it.

I don't use my power to survive, though. Ahh, I do! I use it to go fast to run and run and run, and endure and endure all the hardships that we run through. Maybe that's what my power's for; to run and run and run, and to endure all hardships I run through.

I think power helps to know the difference between hardships and peace. I think power brings energy to take on the hardships and to release into peace. I think power brings courage.

I wonder if power brings love. I don't know. It would have to be very gentle power. Then it could. Gentle, loving power. That will heal everything. And take away the mystery. That will tell us how to lead our lives.

Gentle, loving power. Now to find it, and keep it that way.

–JR

HANDSOME HARRY, BURRO, JACK

It's a good day, a really good day. We like the excitement of Thomas coming home. It's a kind of magic that cured his leg. That wouldn't have happened in the wild, and it was something that he might not have been able to adapt to.

Noah and I were fortunate. And, for us, being with humans works very well. It's great to have your food delivered. Our family helped us in the wild with finding food and water. It's interesting how all works out. We were called to a gathering of the big family, not knowing how we would get there, and here we are! Just goes to show that patience, patience and more patience is good. If you're supposed to get there, you will. It is called trust, and yes, it is very hard for humans, but you can do it. Really you can! Thank you.

–W

HANNA, BURRO, JENNY

Humans? Oh... whaa? Oh wait... I've heard of this. Okay, let me get myself together... right! Humans. I like them. They can be good. Most don't understand us. Us animals, I mean. I don't think they do, anyway. They just seem to think we are un-individual. They seem to think that we don't feel or have any preference or anything. I don't see how, because all you have to do is look around at us. We are all different, we are all individual. And we live and breathe and feel and think and sometimes we hurt. Sometimes you humans hurt us. That is not nice. We don't hurt you... well, unless there is cause... well... some animals have been so hurt by humans that they will just try to hurt you on purpose. But none of us here do it. And we would never. Because we are loved here. We are cared for. And those that come into our home (pen) respect us. They look at us with loving eyes. They try to see who we are.

So my message to humans would be to try your best to see who we really are. We are just like you, really. We are really just like you. Tell them that.

Humans should see us animals are the same as them. We are the same. We are just like them. Treat us as you would treat someone you care about. That is what I would like them to know.

–SM

HARLEY, MAMMOTH BURRO, GELDING

It is very important for people to accept who they are without judgment. This was something that I had to learn myself. For a while, I was upset that I was so huge. Other burros around me seemed so much happier than I did—more at peace with themselves.

Then one day I was standing near a person who was thinking very negative thoughts about themselves, and I understood that I was doing a "people thing" by judging myself. Now why would I, an animal, be thinking like a people? I did not want the thought of not liking myself, so I raised both my back legs and kicked it far away from me.

Since that day, I can be happy with myself. I like to follow people around, and be with people, but I don't have to take on any people thoughts or qualities. I stand firm in the Harley center of my being, loving my uniqueness among burros. So I say to people, hug the center of your being.

–CM

HARMONY, HORSE, MARE

Think of life as music. When you get into it, you can flow with it and it becomes beautifully melodious as you participate in making the music of life.

Sometimes life is harsh and dissonant to get our attention. Then it can become soft and harmonious again, like my name.

You can make as much music as you want and make whatever kind of music you want. Sometimes it's by yourself. It's your own music. Sometimes that doesn't fit with everyone else's, but it's just as beautiful. You just must listen to your own music and not let someone else's harm yours.

Sometimes people get pushy with their music. Keep yours intact. Keep it strong and strong and strong and then it will be very beautiful.

Many of us have our own music and we even get lonely with it. We think too much of it being different instead of it being so beautiful in its differentness, instead of noticing its uniqueness and its creativity because it is different.

Your own song is as beautiful as any other song because all music is beautiful. So belt it out! Your own song. Make your music from your heart and in your heart and with your heart. It will open other hearts to be sure.

Because it's so real.

–JR

HEATHER, DOG, FEMALE

(Bark, bark, bark.) Who are you... what do you want? No. I don't have anything to share.
Go away.

–SM

Heather,
Photo by Darlene Stolz

HEATHER, HORSE, MARE

It's been a long haul, the worst is over. Fear is protective until it no longer is. Then it's hard to shed, even if you try hard. It stops you from breathing. What I'm most conscious of now is my breathing. I can breathe again, and breath is life. As you let the fear go, the breath slowly returns. It's as if I can inhale and smell again and feel again. I am Glad I can breathe again and even my body feels lighter. It's scary because letting go is letting in.

My thanks and gratitude (to HDLM) for giving me back my life connection to all that is. It allows me to leave the past behind.

–BG

HENRY, BURRO, GELDING

I represent the father of time, the father of moment, the father of chance. I am here to tell you not to give authority to time. That is my job! For you it is only to enjoy and relax.

Only I can change the time, you cannot! Not until you become a father of time yourself.

How do you become a father of time? Once you have embraced all things in love and energy. Once your first dream alchemizes, once your heart and soul breathes with the Universe in compassion and gratitude, when you become Knowing, then the knowing of how to is yours.

You all have a lot of work to do.

–S

HENRY, BURRO, JACK

For the Human Race, remember that it is not a race in the speed sense. Where are you constantly rushing off to? What can be so important? Stop awhile. Chew some grass. Look around. Observe your surroundings. Do you like them? Are you at Peace? Do you feel your life is whole and complete? What will it take to make it that way? Humans are too busy making demands of themselves and others to stop and question their existence. Not many of them know what their purpose is in the overall scheme of things. Let me tell you. You are here to raise the vibration on this place, to grow spiritually and to connect with yourselves and others through your hearts. My advice to you is to find some quiet time, some quiet space and quiet your mind enough to let your other senses take over for a moment. Think about whether or not you are happy with your surroundings and your life. Are you behaving in a positive way and living from your heart? Reach into your heart space. You will find comfort there and it will show you the way to a joyful existence. Look at me standing here in the sun and chewing grass. To many I may look pathetic and I may draw sympathy from casual observers. Let me tell you I am one of the most content beings there ever was. Want to know why? I live in my heart. I stand on the Earth, but I live in my heart. It's where you should live too. Go there and see. See how all the little details, conflicts and complications of your lives fade away when you are there. Surroundings don't matter so much. What I have or don't have is of little significance. You will feel the same and once you are there, truly, and that is when you will begin to raise the vibration of the Earth and each other. The time is near when this will occur for Humans. We can feel it and some of you can as well. For this we are glad. Your lives will be different very soon.

–CD

HOLLY, DOG, FEMALE

Oh my, what a question! I have lots to share. Where in the world do I start? Start at the beginning.

Well, in the beginning there was earth. The earth was populated by all manner of plants and animals. Some smarter (like us dogs) than others (smile). Well... actually, we are all ancestors of a long lineage and changes in our species. But dogs... or some aspect of dog has always been around. The animals competed in the world and ate each other. Many of them did anyway. Humans came along and competed with the animals. Some, they made friends with, like us. We helped each other and grew to love each other. Some humans and some animals... not so much. Some humans to this day don't love others.

That brings us to now. Now is the time to get together, to love each other, to care for each other. Humans think this whole world is for them. Humans think they should be able to do whatever they want to the earth. Humans think they should get to use and abuse whatever and whoever they want to. This is not how it should be. We (animals and humans) are all on this planet together. We are all learning from each other. We are all in life here together. Why do humans think they get to do whatever they want? We've (dogs) never been able to figure this out.

We are close to humans. We love them. We teach them. Some we cannot get to. Their hearts Are closed. Love is an outward energy. Love is giving. Love is sharing and caring for those around you. Love is sharing and caring for those on the same planet. We have for millennium taught this to humans by our example. Some have learned it, some have not. It is time for humans to "get it" now. Why can't they see what they are doing? Why do they continue to do what they do? We are here as examples.
We love you humans. Why don't you love others as we love you? Tell them now is the time. It is not too late. It is never too late to learn love. Tell them we will not quit. We will be here to help those who are ready to open their hearts. Tell them that.
Will the humans hear me?

–SM

HOPI, BURRO, JACK

I too think it's important to live in the moment.
When you live in the past, you live in your wishes
for things to be different.
When you live in the future, you live in your hopes
for what you want.
When you live in the present, you have the perfect chance
for knowing intimately who you are as a part of the oneness.
There is such a rich life for those who catch themselves trying to live
anywhere but in the present. It really is just a change of mind.
When you look at how burros live in moments of joy,
don't you wish you could do that more too?
When we all do more moments of joy
there are even more moments of joy for us to enjoy together.
It just multiplies our happiness together.

–JG

HOWARD, BURRO, GELDING

My, my... why would I want to do that?
Oh. Well, that is a mildly amusing and peculiar thing to do, isn't it?
Well then, I must contribute, mustn't I?
Alright then. Hmmm... I am flabbergasted, really, to find a place such
as this. It is a very interesting and emotional thing for me to realize
that humans can love as these ones love. I hadn't come across that in
my days upon this earth. I wondered if it were possible. Humans seem
to be in their own worlds, in their own heads all the time. There isn't
much space for others in there. At least, that has been my experience.
Here... well, let's just say that I was pleasantly surprised that people
were not all the same. These ones are still in their heads much of the
time, but somehow... somehow, they shift and come back into their
home place. Their hearts. That's what I call the heart, dear one. My
home place. That is where I reside, even through all my hurts and
horrors. I desire to reside here (in my home place) so that I may live in
peace. It is not peaceful when one resides in the mind, you know. It is
not a peaceful place to be in at all.

–SM

HUBERT, DOG, MALE

What do I NOT want to share? Tell humans to live life to the fullest! To lay down with your belly up to the sky and bask in the sunshine. To explore the earth with reckless abandon (not that I'm the reckless type), but to thoroughly enjoy your day.

People forget at times where the focus really should be. They get lost in paperwork. They forget about the earth under their feet. They get bogged down in ideas on how things should look. It's better to let the sky open up above your head and gaze at its brilliance than get caught up in all that. (Not to say you shouldn't take care of business, but to remember when it's time to put the pen down and to go to bed, enjoy one's sleep and get up and do it all over again.)

I'm a "lay down" kind of dog. I enjoy life from the down position and take it all in. I also greet life with a grin and see sunshine between the clouds. I'm the purist form of optimist there is, when it comes to what we must do. We must live in joy because THAT's the icing on the cake. Everything else falls below that, although it too may be pleasurable.

If I could get a human to lay down beside me on their backs to enjoy life from this perspective, you would rise from that posture laughing and feeling grand. Now just imagine all the world doing it! Can you see people laying beside their farm dogs,

house dogs and dogs of all types, in order to share the beauty and wonder of the grass below their feet and the big sky overhead? How so much happier we'd all be together, rather than just the dogs rising and being in joy, alone. You humans should get your dose of "down" time daily. It's good for the heart and is what makes dogs grin big, like me.

–DT

IRIS, BURRO, JENNY

My how our family grew. And how smart we all are. Making changes head over heels. I loved having all the new family members around. Everybody has such a different personality that it made life so much fun. New babies too. What a joy they were. I'm surely coming back! I want to see more of all of everything. I had headaches sometimes. Eeyore said I had to quit looking at the sun when it was up. But when it came up so beautifully every day I just wanted to watch it as long as I could.

I know we are all Divine. I believe in each and every one of us. This is what I would want everybody to know who doesn't. And that it's easy to believe in each other. You just don't pay any attention to the things that would make you disbelieve. It's the best kind of love we can give each other, don't you think?

–JG

IROQUOIS, BURRO, JACK

What on earth do people really want to know?

Why do people bother with so many things all the time? Having so many things. Changing all the so many things around from there to there. Stacking so many things. Getting more so many things.

That was something that really impressed me in the burro life. We didn't have any, so many things. What we had we shared and we didn't own anything.

This was a real change for me.

I saw why my memory was so overloaded. I had to keep track of all the things I owned and someone else owned. I had a sharp brain for figures and items and as a burro, these memories would keep slipping into my newfound peaceful existence. I guess it was that way every day in that other time. It's sad what we do to ourselves when another choice would be just fine.

Without so many things to take up all my hours, I had the chance to be loved for just me and to love back the same way. I am very grateful for this!

I think that's JUST how it is supposed to be!

–JG

ISABELLA, BURRO, JENNY

My heart has bleeding in it from the sorry of the loss of my old home. I wonder if you have ever lost your beloved home. I do not wish to be critical or ungrateful. I have a very good home and love of the human kind is all over here.

So we have a different environment for learning about life, and we have goodness here and we have each other. We all have loneliness for the land we shared with others who ran free.

I have wonderings about how you see that. I have wonderings if this is an experience we share. I see good hearts here. I don't know if bad hearts exist. I don't think so, maybe just fearful hearts. When hearts are fearful they do things that can be hurtful to others.

I am so sorry that some of you have fearful hearts. Do you hide them from each other? Or from yourself? Do you know you have fearful hearts? These are questions I do not know the answer to. Fearful hearts need love so they don't have to be so fearful. If they don't say they are fearful they can't get or give love. I hope your hearts tell you when they are fearful so you can give love to them and be kind to yourself. Then you can be kinder to others too.

I have a fearful heart. It makes me want to hide. I might bite or kick someone who looks dangerous so I also need to give my fearful heart love. Even if I get it from someone else I must give it to myself as well.

Many of us don't know that. I wonder if it would matter where we live if everyone knew that and if everyone knew how to do that. I am learning that here. My heart got closed in fear, more closed than it ever was. Now it is opening.

I also help to open the hearts of other beings. I see it in their eyes. Some people wear their hearts in their eyes. I like that. I can trust them then. And they are brave because they let their fearful hearts show and then they are not so fearful anymore.

Fear isn't as strong as love, I keep forgetting that. Please help me remember.

–JR

JACK, BURRO, JACK

Well, I'm not much on philosophy. I'm just me. I've got memories of dirty rags to more dirty rags and a few small memories of riches. But the memories I am making now are about comfort. I can be comfortable with myself. It seems to be some of what others are talking about so I guess they are experiencing some of the same. I wish I had hands to read books still. I think if burros lack anything, that would be it in my opinion. I loved to read.

Like I said, I'm not much for a lot of the deeper wisdom talk. But I do think learning to be comfortable with yourself is important. So hands is probably something I took for granted at one time. Now I see how important they were. I guess I'm learning right now about all the things you can do with hands. Or could have done.

–JG

JACKOLYN, BURRO, JENNY

I'd like humans to expand their view of the world,
and see that we're all the same at the core.
There is enough for all. If all learn to share, if all learn
to live in the moment, some won't need to feel the urge to hoard.
And please also do better at sharing your space.
There is room for all if all share. We are very fortunate here,
but many are not. Please visit us sometime.
We'd love to see you.
Thank you.
–W

JAKE, HORSE, GELDING

I have lots I would like to share with humans. Understanding is one of them. Humans need to start understanding that we are all one. Every good act reflects upon one another. For instance, that good understanding energy is passed on with every good deed. It is time to start doing more good deeds and to pay it forward so that more and more good deeds are being done all over the world. This will bring about a new understanding of human nature. There is goodness in this world. It is time for this goodness to grow and grow many fold to all creatures - human and non. As I said one good deed turns into

Jake, Photo by Deb Derr

another which turns into another which turns into another and so on. All it takes is for one human to start thinking a good thought - another will think a good thought- then another and another. See where I am going with this?

Humans are finding this necessary to do at this time. It is time to start doing good deeds in a big way now. Humans are at a turning point. This project here at Hacienda is helping this process along. Animals have so much to teach to humans if they would only listen.

Listening is something else that humans need to start doing more of. Open up their intuition. Listening to their good thoughts - putting them into action. Do only good, say only good, think only good. The world will be such a better place to live if humans start incorporating this into their daily lives.

Love everyone and everything no matter what one does or says to you. Show only love. You will be in such a better place if you do this.

Thank you so much for asking me.

–MM

JASMINE, BURRO, JENNY

Smiles make everything go away. When someone smiles at me it brightens my world. All of a sudden there is nothing between me and that smile. Then I smile back. I can't help it! Try it sometime! When two beings smile at each other it creates an instant kinship and for a moment, unity. You become aware of a silent understanding that there is joy to share. Sweet, attainable joy comes by sharing something as simple as a smile. Hold that place every day for as long as you can. Practice over and over and pretty soon laughter will join you. Your eyes will begin to smile and all you see will come to you in a different light. Nobody can think bad thoughts or do bad things when they are smiling. I like to nudge people so I can show them my smile.

Kick up your heels and play. Feel the Joy. Dance!

All we ever have is the moment we're in. Let that be what carries you through the day. Spend time wisely, for it is short. No sense worrying about the future. Live your life and fill your heart with Love. I do. I don't know of any other way to survive. I am a being of light and all who touch me will feel that light. I infuse them with my energy. It makes people want to be near me and I like it.

I am curious about people and I want to help them. I like to switch my tail and prance and dance because I like the way it makes me feel. Always take the opportunity to do what gives you joy whenever you can.

I love attention from humans. When they take the time to slow down and give me a scratch and talk to me it puts them right there with me in the moment. Then all of the other things like the ugliness of how things can turn out to be fades away. Life becomes uncomplicated and feels good. Even if it lasts just for a moment, the moment is good and lets me know that there is possibility for it to be that way always. Joy is within your reach. Keep adding your moments together and pretty soon you'll find it to be a lifetime. Thank you for taking a moment to talk with me. Maybe others will do the same. There is no anger in animals. We are instinctual and know what we are supposed to do. Even when we are being manipulated by man we remain unchanged. It's nature's written program. Being docile doesn't mean animals have a lesser intelligence. We know everything you're thinking. Manipulation does not change our purpose for being here.

Being of service is what we choose. We are happy in our roles. Jasmine says she likes freedom and the good care she is getting. Burro Love is a powerful force and has been around since Biblical times and even before. They are all one and remain united in Peace and Love. Four hooves give good grounding to Earth.   –CD

JASMINE, DOG, FEMALE

Let's see. I don't know a whole lot about humans, and I wonder about them. I know about you (her persons). I don't know a lot about others.

Humans are a mystery, even you (her persons) are a mystery to me.

How can I understand you? I think it's a good idea for me to understand you. Since all of us occupy the earth.

Do you want to be understood? I think you do. I know you do. Everyone wants to be understood and accepted. So I know something about you already. Because you aren't any different than I am

Ah-ha, we are the same. Well, do you know that? Do you get excited or feel insulted? I think it's neat. Then we don't have to be lonely if we are ever alone, 'cause we are never foreigners... instead, we are always family.

Family is special. That means we love each other and we tolerate each other and we accept each other and we do for each other and we are loyal to each other. And we do all of that all the time no matter what

If we are family together, then that means we are that way with each other. I know lots about that. I think you do, too.

I welcome you all to my family. Ha, now we are a very big family. We don't know each other, even. Well, let's have some small families so we can know each other. I have one already.

One thing I know is to be strong. We are always afraid we aren't strong enough. That's human and that's dog, too.

I wonder why we worry about that? Well, I think so we can exist, so we can be. But we pretend a lot, and maybe if we didn't pretend we wouldn't have to worry about that.

Maybe that's our important work. To stop pretending and to be real. If we are all real, we will all be strong. Because I think it's stronger to be real than to pretend. We pretend when we are afraid and are cowards. We are real when we are brave and strong. That's what allows us to be real, when we have the courage to be real.

Well, it took me a while to get there, but I'm very glad I did! Because I understand me better and you better. And I want to be real with you.

–JR

JASPER, CAT, MALE

I am pretty young, but I suppose I can say something about fun and adventure.

Sometimes life is worth taking chances for the best smell of all. Sometimes it is short, so it better be worth it. But if you are going to sit safely and long for that smell, it'll keep you from living life. So either you better go for that smell, or find another one that you can be full with instead of being all cranky and tight because you can't get to the smell of your dreams.

You have to know what you are doing, and what you are about, to make the best decision. I suppose it's a good idea to know smells and which ones work best for you. I know mine. There are many. The best one is yet to come. I only know it's best when I have been with the bestness

 that I suspected all along.

You know, each smell is the best of all. That's because it really is, and also because you get better at smelling. That's one of the really good things about being on earth, the greatest smells. They just get you all open inside so you can become a part of it.

Do you know about such things? Is it foolishness to you? I hope not. Cats live in a world of smells. That's our world. We learn to live in the human world of thoughts and fast movements and noise. Smells make you peaceful. Come to the cat world and learn about smelling. You can stay as long as you want. There are plenty of smells to go around. Pick your favorite. You will always remember it.

Well, my advice to you is to remember your smells so you remember what you are all about, and so you remember what life is all about.

–JR

JEREMIAH, MAMMOTH BURRO, GELDING

It's about time, I have been waiting for this. First, I would like to say thank you to all beings who are in the now and doing what they can to change, evolve and help.

Secondly, I feel the stress and emotions of all those who are lost and seeking. I say to them come find yourself. Go within, always within is where you will find us and other divine beings to guide you home. Peace to you.

–S

JERICO, BURRO, GELDING

Yes, yes I hear you! I hear you all! Stop your whining and change yourself, your life, your friends, your work and anything else that doesn't make you happy! It is as easy as that.

Only the You makes the choice to make it difficult. You also have the choice to make a change fun and exciting or difficult and hard. Why would you choose the latter?

–S

JEWEL, HINNY, MARE

Hello, my friend! Thank you for asking me to participate. And, thank you for keeping me with Victor James, and thank you for letting us pick our names, instead of those horrible names assigned to us before. Letting us pick our names shows respect for us. The names we pick fit us. Some humans choose very disrespectful names for their animal companions. Others pick names they think are cute. Would they, I wonder, want someone else to name them, or name someone else's baby instead of letting the mother or family name the baby?

Sometimes names are passed down from a family elder. Here one of the babies was given his grandfather's name. That was a wonderful thing, and kept tradition alive. Grandfather took another name when he gave his to his grandson. Our humans waited to learn the name after the family approved the honor. Please honor our choices of what to be called, so that we know you respect us. Thank you.

–W

JIMENY, HORSE, GELDING

The message I have for humans is one of peace, blue skies, and love. Blue skies abound. Just look up and you can see the vastness of them. Enjoy the serenity in those blue skies. Long for their tranquility because you never know when clouds and storms will take over. When the storms and clouds do come - all you have to do is think of those peaceful blue skies, and they will return. Your lives have so many dimensions, just like the sky. Let your thoughts direct the skies in your life. Always strive for the clear blue skies, for they can be so tranquil. Meditate on the big fluffy clouds. They have messages in themselves. Always strive for those peaceful blue skies within.

It helps if you look up to the skies for guidance and help. All you need in life you can find in nature. Take time to let your minds wander to the sky. Breathe in the air. Blow it back up to the sky. Lift your arms up towards that beautiful sky. Twirl around.

> Enjoy the moment.
> Enjoy the moment.
> Peace and blue skies.

–MM

JJ JIMMY JACK, BURRO, GELDING

> Feeling tired, but I keep on keeping on.
> Need to take breaks often.
> Show up and be counted.
> I love being involved and alive.
> Others depend on me to be there for them.
> Gather up what you can so you can save for the future.
> Reserve your energy.
> –LK

JOJO, HORSE, MARE

Take us into your hearts so you know how we feel. Take each other into your hearts so you know how each other feels. We feel that way, too; happy, sad, angry, frightened, and it directs our daily lives like your feelings direct yours.

Our world may be different than yours, but we don't feel any different. Everything we do is so very important to us. Like what you do is important to you. We all have souls... your souls are important to us. I hope ours are important to you. Keeping us in your hearts will keep our souls together. Keeping our souls together can make us so strong, and so much in a beautiful and holy life that we will all burst in joy in a beautiful, holy and healthy world.

Tell your people. You can enjoy each other better then. You can love each other better then. Then the whole world benefits. Does that please you? It makes me happy.

–JR

JOAN, BURRO, JENNY

Being a mother is one of the most important things a person or an animal can be. Our babies are the mothers and fathers of our future. Mother's nourish the future. Our burro babies are all the most perfect expression of being a burro. People do not honor their mothers and respect them enough. Partly this is the human mother's fault, because her role has been disparaged and not valued, so that she is unaware of her greatness.

I feel for the females of humans, because their worth has been stolen from them and taken away by the men. This is shameful. Mothers protect life and teach the young ones how to respect them and all that lives and breathes on the earth. The ground I walk upon is the mother to all of us. Husbands and fathers must prize the woman above all else for her great gifts to humankind. I say to human men, respect the women in your lives for all men are born of a mother. A burro is born instinctively knowing this; and mother, father, and baby live the truth of this every moment. We are grateful.

–CM

JOSHUA, BURRO, JACK

Hello my brother. I do want to share for this book . I am well again, and what I want to share is this. I have lived many physical lifetimes on the receiving end of abuse and neglect on the part of human kind. And I just left my physical body at the end of one of the worst physical

Peanut: Photo By Lecia Breen

lives ever, and yet, and the end, I found myself in a place of miracles, of truly unconditional love, compassion, and empathy. And thank you, not one bit of pity. I was accepted as a complete and perfect being, even though I had my doubts about that myself. And that is what matters. Please share all of this, and do not be embarrassed. You are supported and encouraged by loving humans, those truly helping you with this labor of love you do, those helping with the book, the Council, and all the non-human beings there. They are greatly appreciated, and without you, my brother, none of this would be. I've shared my heart with you, and I know you will keep that conversation to yourself, and every being who resides there, or who has resided there, or who is yet to reside there, know what I shared with you.

To all humans, please learn and understand what this incredible group of humans is doing, and teaching, and living. If you all learn unconditional love, and that we are truly all one, all will be perfect. It is only now, after my returning to pure spirit, that I see what this place is. I was too much in pain and sorrow while I was there. The new world is upon us, and it is at this place of miracles. I can now give all of you my unconditional love, and I do. I am free to do that, and I do.

–W

JUSTIN, BURRO, JACK

The state of the earth is deplorable. Humans are at fault. It's sad to say, but you are insatiable. You have, yet you want; you get, yet you throw away. You need to learn to savor the important things in life. You need to direct your attention to what is necessary for sustaining life, not what would be nice at the moment, which changes in the next moment.

It is vital that you take a deep breath and come to your senses. It is not necessary to have more, to be faster, to do better. It is necessary to have enough, to take your time to enjoy the moment and to do well enough – that is all that is necessary. It is so simple I cry at the wastefulness of your desires. It is not only unnecessary, but also self-destructive, to want for yourself to the exclusion of the greater good.

Take what you need, every bit of what you need, and leave all of what you do not need for others. This way there will be water enough for all life, food enough to feed everyone who hungers, air enough to breathe and land enough to support us.

This is not all there is to relate on this subject, but it is more than enough for you to ponder as you make your way through life.

I would like to share the wisdom of the wildlife all around for I have heard them speak. They remind us all to partake of the gift of life in singularity while respecting life in plurality. You are one, each is an entirety, complete and perfect, yet all are connected and interwoven in life. Respect for all things brings fulfillment to self, whether you have two legs, four, eight, or none.

I speak for all who live in this haven of miracles when I say gratitude surrounds you and blankets you against the cold, shades you from the sun's hot rays and provides sustenance for your heart.

–JGIL

JYNGA, BURRO, JENNY

Oh. Ha-ha. That is a funny question. Well... I think I might have something to share. Hmmm... well... let's just say that it is important to love your life. You know, the life you are living is one that you have chosen. It is, of that I am sure.

I chose this life. I chose this place. I chose everything about it. I don't think humans remember the time before time. I mean, the time before they came here (to earth), the time before they were born. I don't believe they do. We do.

I remember waiting for my time to come here. And I am so happy to be here! I am in love with my life. I think that is a good thing to say to humans, for them to love their life. They chose it, so why not enjoy it fully, yes? Get right into in and involve yourselves. Express and create and dream and love... oh, that is the most important quotient, love. Go for it. Go for your life! And you will see, once you fully allow your life into you, into your very beings, that it is the most perfect place for you.

Ha-ha... that's funny. Your life is the most perfect place for you! That's what I want to share with humans!

–SM

JYNGO, BURRO, JACK

Sometimes our life is very difficult.

Sometimes our life is very easy, smooth and comfortable.

But eventually each of us must die a death that causes us to let go of a world made up of our senses.

Everywhere there are challenges to wake us up. Sometimes these challenges are so tiring. When we get tired of doing our own challenges we take a break and begin to look around at others. We see everyone is going through the same kind of conflicts that challenge them to die. Maybe that's why some would rather create constant conflict. They are afraid to die.

It is an old but very true saying, "It is a good day to die". I think more people should try to understand just what this really means and could mean in their life. Be brave. You can only get better.

–JG

KING SOLOMON, BURRO, GELDING

Please dearest humans, please I ask of you to reach into your hearts and hold it alight to yourself. Hold you hearts up and out and see the beauty that resides therein. That is you, dear humans. You are not mind, not body... you are hearts... and souls.

Once you can see, feel and be your very own hearts, then your soul can come forth. And your souls have much to share with you. Your very own souls have you to teach you. That is who you truly are, dearest humans. You are soul. Reach within yourselves to find it. It is there waiting for you.

–SM

KNIGHT OF DREAMS, HORSE, GELDING

I have seen much in the World and many Worlds. I have come here for a purpose as we all have. Frankly, it can be a hard road with you humans. Can you not see the beauty in life, instead of concentrating on the destruction? Your life has a purpose as all beings do, do you know what it is? Are you following your heart? Make changes now, don't wait for the little time to change.

–S

KYRO, BURRO, JACK

Based on everything I've seen and heard, we're all pretty lucky people to be here sharing our life with each other. Sharing or being with others is an unfolding process throughout our life. I wanted to know just what we do with it.

I think I can explain it best by saying we take it personally. We take each other personally. We're always testing what we're told and examining it in the context of our life. If we don't think about things and decide if it's true for me, will this help me, can I use it today, can I appreciate it; we become just another dependant follower. We never will get to know the person inside us. I'm doing pretty good here. Thank you for having me.

–JG

LACEY, HORSE, MARE

Humans can be very thoughtful and sweet or mean and arrogant, it depends on 'why' makes them. They need to learn their souls are light and will go back to light. They come from light and will go back to light. All this time here is for training and learning. There's no need to be arrogant or mean cause later, we all become light again and will all be the same. Except those here who are sweet and good – their souls will be even lighter once they leave here.

When we're all here on this land we're here to learn, laugh and love. That's – in the end – all the matters. Love!!

I'm happy now. I wasn't always happy, but this is the way it is supposed to be. I was meant to be unhappy and be with unkind humans for a while. Now I'm here, both to learn and teach humans to be kind, happy and at peace. They also need to take time to be still and take in all that is around them. That's how we all should learn. We all have a light and dark side while here. We have to let the light side out more often and then the dark side will go away or at least get not as dark.

Most of all 'love'; humans should never forget that. Love, hugs, pats – all are beautiful. That's all I have to say.

–LT

LANCE, BURRO, GELDING

Life is a game. Don't take it so seriously. I have noticed that humans tend to be very serious about everything. They need to laugh at themselves more with a big, burro hee-haw. Like this, 'HEE-HAW!' That was a very loud one.

I highly recommend that they eat gingersnap cookies, too. Gingersnap cookies always make me feel little laughs inside. Of course, if they do not like gingersnap cookies, then humans must eat or do something that makes them feel little laughs inside. I say that they must do one thing every day that makes them feel little laughs. Life will start to go better for them. Laugh your way through life with a big HEE-HAW-HAW-HAW!"

–CM

LARRY, BURRO, GELDING

Yes. Humans. Many don't seem to recognize themselves in others. What I mean is that most humans look outside of themselves and see another. What they are really seeing is their own reflection, their own self. They don't realize this. It is true because we are all one spirit and there is no separation between spirit. We individualize, yes. But we are not separate from each other. We are not "other" spirits. We are not "from another spirit". We are all from the same spirit, therefore, we are one and the same. We are one.

That is probably, the most important thing humans might like to learn. Because without doing so, they will continue on the same, same path that they are now existing on. And many humans are merely "existing". They are not "living". They walk around life reacting to and judging those outside of themselves, but they are only reacting and judging themselves. They are seeing parts of themselves they do not like through their own filters.

Ah ha. You wonder how I know this. Well, I have been around. I am more than meets the eyes, so to speak. You are not surprised by my words, but you do wonder. Most humans, when they read my words, will not believe it comes from me. But it does. Do you know why? Because I am no different than they are. I am of the same spirit. Spirit cannot be separated, only individualized. There... that is my message to humans.

Say thank you to those who care for us. We love them. They are the best of the humans.

Bless them. Thank them. We do.

–SM

LAWRENCE (ONE WHO LOVES), BURRO, GELDING

Oh yea!!!!!!!!
Life is a time for JOY!
Celebrate your life.
–RK

LEGACY, HORSE, MARE

My sense of peace in my heart is deep. I have a special place within me that I hold for your species- can you sense it? My message begins from the early onset of my time (from her physical birth). When my brain was new and impressionable, and yet I recalled the basic truths that permeate through all things. The sense that we are One is in fact the biggest Truth but let me not linger here as others will breach this subject. There is also the power of togetherness. Living in a herd, we seek shelter and annointance with one another. By "annointance" I mean having the highest regard for all beings within our space and those beyond our vision. My name is Legacy for a reason. It was not just strewn out of a hat. It's a very prophetic name. I have wisdom between my ears and the patience to share it with any who ask. The grass below our feet wiggles with life. It is a vibrant glow that sheds itself too fast in its physical form before it lingers and dies, only to come again with the rain. And yet the vibrance within did not perish. Only the grass blade that held it's brilliance for a time.

The vibrance that makes up the grass strands is new and yet not so. It sings to us in all its newness and growth and we take a moment to sing with it, appreciating the vibrance in which we are all a part. My messages is clear. I want people to trust what they know. To turn inward and look for that very place hidden in which they once remembered what I am talking now about. Within each particle is life. Vibrant life. It is not just pulsating, it is glowing. Your heartbrims would be overflowed with joy if you knew this. Wynne knows this as do those that dwell here. Animals on the planet know what I speak. Hear me loud and clear, all life takes different forms and yet each is as precious as the little grass seed of which I speak. Vibrance doesn't come in different forms, as its essence remains the same. That is my message.

I am a 'sky watcher'. That is me by nature. They do good here, I am pleased.

–DT

LEO, BURRO, GELDING

Why yes I do. I would love to share with humans.

Dear humans:

Thank you for this opportunity to share my wisdom. You may not think I have much to share, being an other, but I do. I live my life and I see things. I know things. I know many things. I am wise to the bone. My being knows. Your being would know too if you just felt it. Feel your own wisdom in your bones. You know more than you think you do. That is, quite honestly, part of your problem. The trick is to feel it in your bones. Not to think about it.

Now... try it. You can do it if you try. Feel those bones of yours. Go inside yourself. Feel. Listen to what wisdom is shared. It is simple really. Feel your way to knowing. Feel your way to knowing yourself. Do you think that we don't know ourselves? We spend a lot of time doing just that. We know ourselves. Because we feel. You can too. Then.... how shall I say, you wouldn't think you know so much (smile).

–SM

Jasmine:
Photo By
Lecia Breen

LESTER, MAMMOTH BURRO, JACK

Where isn't there bounty? In your hearts? Why do you add boundaries and fences that hinder your ability to love? What purpose do they serve except to put obstacles in your way? Tear them down and let go of your fear of judgment from others. It is only their fears that make them judgmental. Why wall yourself in? When you place boundaries there are two sides. You cannot be your true self and share the abundance of your love and others cannot reach you with what they have to offer to you.

What purpose do boundaries serve except to keep you trapped and in fear of not having enough? What you're trying to protect is your vulnerability. Be vulnerable – it's OK. Trust that love abounds. Like attracts like and loving souls attract other loving souls. There is nothing to fear. Go beyond your boundaries – push – take a chance. It's the only way to make a change. Not just in your life, but in the lives of all whom you touch. There are so many, that in one day just one person can touch so many others. And keep doing that every day and your life will become bountiful and abundant. Share your gratitude and let it be known that you are thankful for even the smallest things in your life. Think about all the parts of your life where you are blessed. I'm sure every one of you will have a very long list.

Think of these things daily and let them be the source of your joy. Soon it will be impossible to keep all of it bottled up. You'll find you must share it and others will share with you.

Bounty and Abundance and Joy are my wish for you. That you all begin to recognize that your lives are brimming over with it and all you have to do is remove the veil of your own misconceptions of what is truly important in this life. To be here and to fully appreciate and experience each other is where the blessing begins. Open your hearts to one another. Respect the journey of others and share your experiences with a true willingness to listen. For each time you do that you'll find something in the message from another that will help you on your journey through this life. It is from others that we learn and grow. We cannot do this if we shut them out by placing boundaries. None of us are meant to travel alone. We are here together for a reason and a purpose. Unite in Love and it will all become clear.

Carole: *Do you have anything else you'd like to share?*

Lester: Beware of the cactus and its pricklies.

Carole: *What does that mean?*

Lester: It means watch your step from Burro perspective.

Carole: *Do you mean literally or figuratively?*

Lester: It means both, but also be aware of what will befall you if you don't watch where you go. In other words, make clear your intentions before you start off on a journey. Know where you are going. Even if it changes along the way, at least start out by knowing where it is you'd like to go.

Carole: *Is there anything else?*

Lester: Sunshine is the best thing on the planet but too much can harm you so make sure you get some shade too.

Carole: *Any personal experiences you'd like to share?*

Lester: I was once a pack mule in the desert and have gone for days without water. The desert is a strange place to be. If you ever want to experience nature in its barest elements then that's where you should go. There is a strange beauty to the barren landscape and sounds galore. Here the animals are wary and swift. For survival, all precisely intertwined and willing to endure the elements to live in this place. Being there allows you to experience what it is like if time stopped and yet, time in the desert stretches forever, unchanged. You'll never run out of new things to look at and nature's palette is truly amazing. It has a uniting force that includes humans as well. When survival becomes the focus/intent things change. We all become united in purpose. All other thoughts escape and we become who we truly are in the purest form.

–CD

LETA, BURRO, JENNY

Oh.... I have humble words. I have nothing to say of consequence.

I wish for everyone to know of their own humility. I know of mine. And, sometimes I don't know and I have to trip over it to become aware again.

Hmm.... well, what else to say about humility? I think it's noble. I think it's noble to know we are all the same and of equal importance. I think it is refreshing to know that. It refreshes me and actually makes me feel proud of my humility.

Isn't that a hoot! To be proud of humility. Maybe I'm not as humble as I think. You see, it can be so very subtle. I am very glad I noticed that. Humble is a quiet place to be and so peaceful, because no competition is necessary. We feel such a connection into our unity, into our oneness, into our togetherness, into our consciousness. We are elevated then spiritually and it brings such joy.

So humbleness is strength and it takes us far, much farther than we can imagine we will go. We do not have to be locked into dullness. Humbleness and simplicity are not dull. They leave wide open spaces for viewing what is beautiful and good and growing. They leave wide open spaces for learning and growing and for being thrilled beyond belief.

Do not underestimate humbleness. It is glorious and has so much room. Mostly it has room for love, for loving yourself and for loving others. Mostly it has room for the fullness of love.

–JR

LICORICE, CAT, FEMALE

When I'm in a tree do not mistake me for a bird. I eat them.

When a bird is in a tree do not mistake it for a cat. It is afraid of me.

Always know and accept and honor us and each other for what we are and who we are and not for what you want us to be.

We are angelic beings as you are, and we are who we are. Maybe we can change. I don't know that. Maybe you can change. I don't know that. Maybe it's a good, kind idea for us all to change to more kindness and compassion. I think so. I don't know how. I know some of us do. My heart listens to them to see if I can follow. Perhaps I can, even with human help.

But first you must help yourselves. First you must change yourselves so you know what you are talking about when you ask us to be different. First you must bring more compassion into your lives and love in service to others instead of to only yourself. How kind a world we would have if we all thought about service to others even just 1 hour daily.

I might do that. It's a cat meditation. Maybe you can try it as a human meditation. Then we can both feel kindness and love well up inside us and be joyful forever.

–JR

LILY, DOG, FEMALE

One thing we can teach humans is to waggle more. We have a built in waggle, and I think humans have lost their waggles, but only they've forgotten they have it in the first place.

Waggling opens many doors. Everyone loves a good waggle. Even when someone gets mad at you, all you have to do is waggle and you are forgiven.

I bet if you look hard enough you will find your waggle and if you wish hard enough, you will grow a tail to waggle with. Some creatures in my people don't have tails either. My mother told me that. She told all of us. The first thing she did when we came out was to lick us clean and dry. Then she looked to see if we had a good tail, and she breathed a big sigh and said "they will have beautiful waggles".

Sometimes we become so excited we become a waggle. Not just any waggle mind you. Our very own waggle.

Sometimes we over waggle and then we get scolded. There's never too much waggle, I say. Can't ever waggle too much. Waggling too much doesn't hurt anyone. My humans know this. The secret is out. Hey don't know about their waggles either.

Hope they find them.

I hope you find yours.

It's a bit of a project when you don't have one to begin with

Don't feel bad. You can waggle your arms or your legs or your head, or even your tongue.

Whoops, I don't know about tongues. I think that might not be so good.

Well, anyway, find your waggle. It's a good place to live: in your waggle. Then you get everything you need to live in the world.

Can you imagine that? From a simple little waggle.

–JR

LOBO, BURRO, JACK

Sometimes everybody makes life so complicated. I think it should be kept simple. At least this is something that has been passed down to me. Keep your teaching and learning simple. That way you have time to enjoy your life while you live it. It really is pretty simple.

Look around you and get rid of what you don't need. Organize what you keep so you can use it. Talk about what you do and who you are with excitement. Tell everybody how grand life is and how glad you are that they are here. I think you'll start turning some heads and getting people to thinking. Cause they're going to want what you have.

–JG

LOLA, HORSE, MARE

I just want to say life on this planet is exactly what you make it. No matter what is going on around, we can choose to be happy or sad. Even when abused, there's some beauty in something, we just have to learn to find it. That's my way of thinking. And if I know that, and I'm just a horse (a very advanced 'horse' spirit granted, but still a horse) then humans need to know that and understand it too.

When our stomachs hurt because not enough food, there's beauty in the pain. The beauty is we're still alive, although at times being alive on this earth isn't the best thing. While here, it's hard (harder for humans than for us) to remember what it's like on the other side. And some of us will be very grateful to get back to the other side. But only the high spirit knows what's absolute best, so all spirits need to accept what is happening around them and be happy with what is.

Now, here I have enough food, my belly doesn't hurt, people pat and hug and brush. Life on this side doesn't get any better than it is now. I'm thankful for this and rejoice. I look at the sky, feel the wind and joy in all things around me. Humans need to be this way also. Then all would be happy. And that's it!! That's what you need to know.

–LT

111

LORD JIMMY, BURRO, GELDING

All moments are planned according to the Universe.
We honor this.
People try to escape from themselves
and we want them to know that the true escape is
reaching within and seeing how you have aided in the creation
of our society, our Earth. Now what are you going to do (about it)?
–S

LOREN, HORSE, GELDING

Freedom. That's what I want to say to people.

Freedom is very important to horses. We were put on the earth to run and play. I feel it in my bones when I need to run. When the wind blows, I want to run with it, the two of us together. People get this same feeling in their bones—this need to have time to be free.

When I look at people, I see ropes attached to them. Some people have many twisted ropes, and some have only a few. Freedom is being able to untie your ropes if only for a little time. I see big things attached to the end of people's ropes like their riding wheels (cars), and I sometimes see a barn where they live (a house). I even once saw a box where people put their foods. This person was as big as the box and ate many foods from his box. He was tied to this box, but I could tell it made him unhappy. Sometimes, people have dark, foggy clouds (worries) at the end of their twisted ropes. I shake my head in bewonderment. I try to talk to them, telling them to cut their ropes so that they can be "horse free," but they hear only horse sounds and not my urgings. Please tell them that I am urging them to run with the wind a little every day. Cut your ropes, my people love.

–CM

LORETTA, BURRO, JENNY

I believe we can all ambulate together. That's a big thing for me, ambulating. I like to get around. I never have. I never have had really big space like my relatives. I've always been confined like now. I wonder about this ambulating business. I do have some space now. And it's safe space. Still not like I hear from my relatives. They went to sleep in different places every night. I sleep in the same place every night. It's O.K. I'm curious.

I ambulate with my mind. And I see pictures of hills and green and red and brown and yellow and blue, and all colors that my heart knows are beautiful.

That's glorious. Even more glorious is the feeling of wind and the different smells; smells from the air so we know who has been there, and who is coming. Feelings around our feet, softness, hardness, sinking, tickling. Even more glorious is the feeling of sun on my body in wide open spaces.

The sun is bigger there, lots bigger. It permeates to my bones and makes me feel warm all the way inside them.

I even like rain. I know what that feels like without ambulating with my mind. I like to know what it feels like where my relatives live. I know that, too, because I ambulate with my mind. All alone and free.

I fly in my mind. I breathe and breathe and inhale all the delicious experience of my land. My land, my home, where I have never been. Where I shall never be.

I ambulate in my mind. I thank Spirit for my mind so I can ambulate. I thank you, Spirit. I thank you.

–JR

LOU, LLAMA, GELDING

As there are stars in the heavens, I have that many numbers of questions to ask of you, fellow beings. Alas there is not time enough for that. I do wish to speak of solitude and the graciousness that comes along with it.

In solitude there is peace. In peace there is nature. In nature there is "WE." All beings.

Peace has many components. There are those that "are" peace, those that "practice" peace and those that simply "want" peace, but have no means to find it.

Those that seek peace run in circles. In laps, round and round again as if looking scatterbrained here or there for that which they cannot find. It's because peace is not some jewel lay strung along the ground. It is something within. A hidden jewel, some might say.

I am a proponent of that which can cure our planet. I am one of the beads on a string reaching out to take your hand and pull you in. So that you too can be a bead, strung along the path of peace. But many do not seem to know they have hands in which they can outstretch. It is just so. We cannot pull them in without hands.

And so we wander amongst those with outstretched hands, searching and puling in who we can. The string of peace gets wider, heavier and more secure. It is a colorful web and something we call our own for we are the makers of its width.

The only way to obtain the hands in which you can outstretch is to BE the peace within.

People tend to get caught up in everyday events and are thus are like blinders, getting in their own way. You can't see beyond blinders (I get an image of dark eye blinders like often see on racehorses) with the near expanse as you can see without them. They hinder you and block your progress. Daily events are just that, daily events. Happenings. Comings. Goings. But they are not YOU.

There is a distinction that must be made between you and your daily events. You are not those. You are separate from them. They do not take on the flesh that you hold. THEY (daily events) do not have hands!

To find peace, sit by a lazy river and go within. The lazy river is just a metaphor for your outer existence. Bask in the peace that surrounds you. Search and find it, if you must, but dwell next to it, then allow it to enter you. And there you will find your own peace. Take hold and find that the two are really one. There is peace within and outside of you. It is one peace. And extension, really. Do you not understand?

When you have brought this peace HOME within who you really are, you are no longer a seeker. You have changed into a "be-er". A being of peace. or it dwells within you. Like you've awakened it within your very being, brought it out, brushed it off and made it sparkle. This sparkles out for all to see (though not all will notice it within you) and you will call out for hands to hold and pull in other beings wishing to join the path of peace. Am I understood?

Ask yourself if you are the "seeker", the "be-er" or the wanting of the one of peace, for there is a difference, a big one. To be the seeker keeps you seeking. To be the be-er has you BEING. To be the wanter, keeps you seeking. There is only one end. Only one way to join the path of peace. Be the peace. Be it.

Danielle: *Is there anything else you'd like to share?*

Lou: There are a great many things I wish to share. How much time do we have?

Danielle: *Whatever you wish to add, you are welcome to.*

Lou: Then in that case let me pronounce who I am. I am a very important part of this sanctuary. I feel like the energy vortex or the mediator in which all things meet. Things have to be up to my standards. I expect much out of you, mankind. You are the rain barrel and you need to catch your fill.

We animals already have full rain barrels. We already know our purpose here and our place within. You are like children, tinkering with your utensils and scrambling about, some of you forgetting why you have come and thus not even trying to catch rain!

Danielle: *(He sighs but gives a wise smile.)*

Lou: You will grow and let go of the old ways and pick up your rain barrels and join in with the rest of us beings. It has been foretold.

The rain barrel represents your flesh and spirit. The rain represents that which you fill yourself with. Wealth of happiness. Pure joy. Experience this and you'll find your way back quicker to that which you strayed from. That is all. It is enough.

–DT

LOVE, BURRO, JENNY

I chose the name 'Love" because I wanted all who know me to experience what I have been given. I have been given 'LOVE' and I came into this world to share it with others, particularly humans. That is why I am in the body of a burro. This body was a servant to Christ and Mary and it continues to serve humanity out of pure LOVE. It was my choice to come to HDLM. I wanted to become more visible so I could get my message to as many as possible. My deepest thanks to Wynne and all those who care for us here at HDLM! Mac is right! More miracles are coming and it will all be joyous! It is all LOVE! Just as Mac said—for those of you humans who chose to see our situations as miserable, know that we don't see it that way. We know these situations will bring greater awareness to humans and it is only by touching the emotions of humans that true change will come about. Some of your kind already know that by reaching people at their emotional level is the best way to sell things, goods or ideas. So tell people to rejoice when they can feel empathy for our plights here, for that is truly the beginning of change. My message is that "all", and I do mean "all", is LOVE! (even the misery). Those who can see it, can see the bigger picture. In order to do that, one must be in a higher consciousness. The great thing about being in higher consciousness is that the individual is then free to make choices that they might never have thought of. Of course, the good thing about that is that is when Mother Earth is seen as a valuable player in each of our lives. When that happens, humans will change in their treatment of their land, their water and their air.

So do not despair for us and for what we have been through, for we have willingly chosen to be part of this huge change taking place in human consciousness today. I bring "LOVE" and with that comes "LIGHT" and then follows "JOY". Rejoice with me for I am truly joyous today!

–LB

LOVES LIFE, HORSE, MARE

Wow, thank you. It is a great privilege to be part of this magnificent project. It will heal many, many hearts. It will change many, many minds. It will assist in bringing those who are ready, those with open-hearts, those who are ready to crack open their hearts, into our world. It is wonderful! It is wonderful! It is wonderful! As you can see, I am very excited. I am excited to be a part of it, and excited to witness the unfolding of the love waves as they make their way around the world. Thank you.

Now, dear humans. Dear wonderful, magnificent humans: We the animals of this world love you. We seem to love you more than you love yourselves. We certainly love you more than you love us. And that is another lesson.

Now, Dear humans: Please look after our planet. We live here too. We spend much more intimate time with her and would like her to be happy. She is not happy. Our lives depend on her being happy. So I ask of you to please look after her. Stop and think what it is you are doing. Don't go on and on and on in your lives without thinking what you are doing. Are you in a trance? It seems to be that way. Stop, look and listen to what you are doing to our earth. We rely on her to help us live. We all need to breathe in her sweet, sweet wind. We all need to eat from her very body. We all need to look up into the night sky to dream. How can we all do this if the earth is dirty and smelly and dusty? We can't, can we? We would like to ask you to take better care of her. We would like to ask you to take better care of yourselves. Then, it is hoped you would take better care of us. As a whole, I mean. Take care of all those upon the earth. Us. You. We. We is another name for One. We is Us. Us is One.

See humans? We are all in this together. Take care of yourselves. Be who you are. Let the earth be who she is without you messing her up okay? We are who we are. We love ourselves. You need to love yourselves. Then everything else will fall into place.

Stop, look and listen. And love yourselves. I do.

–SM

LUCY, HORSE, MARE

I have found My Love.
This I never expected.
It is never too late.
When my nose touched his soft, warm nose,
I recognized myself and saw all my beauty
through the majesty of another.
The hours spent with him have magnified my joy.
I wish this for all peoples, that they should see their beauty
reflected in the soul of a true companion.
That alone is worth the seeking and the wait.
For the first time I can say I am truly happy.
–CM

Ranger and Lucy's First Meeting.
Photo by Marge Dreher

LUNA, HORSE, FILLY

I am much more to humans than meets the eye. I am more than a pretty horse. Humans do not see many as a really am. Many of them. I am a being in physical horse-shape, true. And yet I am much more.

Don't let your eyes deceive you. I am more than a physical being of flesh and bone. My body is only a careless measure and not comparable to my soul.

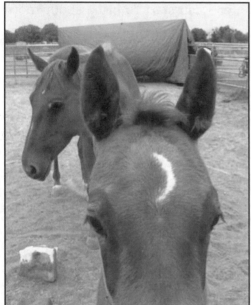

Luna with Mom Trudie.
Photo by W. Zaugg

We are all much more than we appear.

There are burros here who are ancient beings. Almost "saint-like". They are caretakers. More in tune with the land beneath their feet. I am not one among them, though my purpose is clear.

I am to bring forth the message that there are others of my kind in hot pursuit. Others of my kind fleeing your (human) ways so as to be free to be the beings they are. We do not own one another. We own ourselves.

I am clearly respected here and not forced into a mold. I am my own horse. There is a sense of freedom in that. To know that. To exist as that. Thank you.

I dream of how things could be. I would like to extend how things are in my space here at Hacienda to the other horses of the world. In case they yearn for an experience more like my own. Some do. Others do not.

I revel in my own existence. And so I am. Content to be me. Free to live as I choose.

–DT

MAC, BURRO, GELDING

I have learned much in this body and I will be working in the spirit world to help all of you even more. There is a lot more I can do to aide all of you and particularly Wynne and HDLM. I will not forget my friends here. Such kindness I have never known! The sooner they release me from my body, the sooner I can start to bring about more miracles for this shelter and many others. All of this focused attention on us animals who are in need of help, love and attention is going to cause a surge (like a tidal wave) to keep this from happening to animals ever again. As awareness increases, then humans will seek to be better and do better and they will then manifest better. This is not to blame anyone, but it is to help with future manifestations by avoiding the creation of situations that brought each of us here.

My body may be crippled but my soul sings of joy because not only are my days about over in this body, but the days of needing shelters to care for us will soon be gone. Tell them, all of them, that this misery they see is really the birth of better things to come for all of us!

–LB

MADALYN, BURRO, JENNY

LOVE
TOTAL
UNCONDITIONAL
COMPLETE
FOR
YOU!
–W

MAE, BURRO, JENNY

Well, it is important for each individual to know themselves. I mean, to know what they like and want and need. It's also important for an individual to follow their own council, not someone else's. I'm guilty of not doing that and I'm not happy or proud of my life so far. However, I see HDLM as a place to regroup and start again. I think it's important for people to know that no matter what they have done, today they can start new by making changes in their own lives. I haven't been able to always pick my home, but I've always been able to decide how I was going to face the day.

My last situation was bad, but I made it through it to being here at HDLM by choosing to know that better days were coming and I didn't give up. I kept my mind focused on the home I wanted for myself. Everyone can do that, and by choosing attitudes that are positive and that are creating, we all can change our world into a sustainable world for us all. I'm going to do a lot of dreaming and thinking so that my new home is exactly what I want this time!

–LB

MAGNIFICENT, BURRO, GELDING

Not to take our land would be one thing. There are many disgruntled shadows that have blown over the plains in regards to this. We hold not to this type of disgruntlement, and yet there it is, unchanged.

My thoughts are one with yours, let peace thrive and hold not stake on land. It belongs to all. My essence is of earth energy. I love the feel of the dirt below my feet just as you welcome grit under your bare feet.

The earth has many healing properties contained within it. Let it be a salve for your aches and misguided direction.

There is also that humans need to be more like me and my kin- we recognize the birthing of changes within our community of beings. You largely ignore the fact that the very wind blows below your nose. We lift our heads to the breeze in grace. It is wonderful. Do the same and be more like us. You will regain your footing. I will lead you. Ask me anytime. I have seen much and can offer good trail (a way in which to walk).

The wind of change is near. I watch the sky for it. Just as I watch for the summertime. My needs are few. Go now.

–DT

MARABELLE, BURRO, JENNY

This book is important to us. We hope it becomes important to you.
We share our thoughts openly and once one has listened and read this
book they will open to others around them that will speak.
I only ask, is to listen with your heart not your mind. We already know
what's in your mind! It's time to share hearts. Thank you to all that
have chosen to hear.

–S

MARCUS, MULE, GELDING

It's about mountains. It's about friends. You can move mountains
with friends. I look at this mountain a lot, almost daily. Keep it short
and sweet; get to the crux of the matter; keep to the point...don't
waste. Just move through life and keep it uncomplicated. You don't
need a lot – just a friend and a place to sleep and food to eat...good
company. Keep it simple, keep it to a minimum. The rest is a waste and
unnecessary. And I've got it all.

–BG

MARCY, HORSE, MARE

My message is about sadness. I feel sadness all over. I don't know even where it comes from. It seems to float in the air. Where does it come from?

I have been sad. I am at peace now. Life gets better after sadness. Sometimes sadness says "life can be better if you let me be here, so you can leave the part that isn't working, the part that makes you sad." Sadness does that.

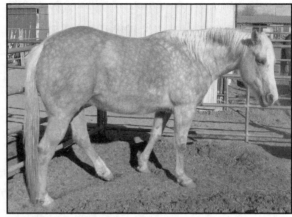

Photo By Lecia Breen

Life is better. I don't like sadness. But I get hopeful when I feel it, because I know that, oh my goodness, I think things are getting even better than ever before. Can you imagine that?

I think sadness makes us alert. You, too. Just makes us wake up to something that hurts us. I feel so sad I want to push it all away. Sometimes I can and sometimes I can't.

You are your own bosses, so I bet you can easy.

I am my own boss of my own soul, so I can help my soul find peace even when there is sadness.

When sadness comes, it gives us exercise in hoping and making things better because we have to. Or sadness could make us die in our spirit.

You know, by goodness, sometimes we have to die a little to get happy again.

My sadness has taken me to peace. I am happy now. I hope yours does too.

–JR

MARGARITA, BURRO, JENNY

It's cold outside. Anytime when it's cold outside, we have to find warmth in a huddle with each other. And if we find warmth in a huddle with each other, we can even find warmth inside. And if we find warmth inside, we might even find warmth for each other.

Oh, dear, that might be dangerous. What if we love someone who becomes our enemy? Well, if we are really strong and close to our spirits, maybe we can even find warmth for our enemy. Have you ever done that?

Neither have I. Interesting concept. Might be worth trying. Anyone interested? If you are, tell me, and maybe we can have warmth for each other. Maybe we can even love each other. Maybe then we will find out if we are enemies or friends. Maybe warmth will tell us. Maybe warmth will make a difference. Maybe warmth will make our feelings different. I don't know how to handle that. I'll bet you don't either.

Maybe we can help each other find out.

–JR

MARIA, BURRO, JENNY (IN SPIRIT)

What we choose, you also choose.
What we see, you can also see.
What we feel, you can also feel.
It is about making the choice in your life, in your being
to draw your soul's purpose and journey into present space.
This is where we stand (in present space).
This is where we wait for you (in present space).

–S

MARIA, BURRO, JENNY

I have a leeriness of anyone different. I give them chances. It takes a long time for me to trust. I don't hurt anyone unless they hurt me. Please don't hurt us. Please don't hurt anyone. Please honor us all. Please honor everyone. It takes very little to do that. Maybe patience. Maybe some love too. You don't have to love us a lot. Maybe just love life, and all the spirits in life. Maybe then you'll love your own spirit, too. Maybe then you'll love your own life more.

I don't know how it all happens. Just find that love, I guess. I have to find it too. Because sometimes I lose trust, and then I lose love. I can't get love if I don't trust. You probably can't either.

Maybe deep inside, though. Maybe that's all where it is. Deep inside. Deep inside.

–JR

MARIA ELENA, HORSE, MARE

My dear, I have much to share with humans, with the human race. It is an interesting term, is it not? Human race? Ahhh… because some of the humans think there really is a race.

Let me share something with them: there is not. There is no race. That is where they get into trouble, thinking there is somewhere they need to be, something they need to do, something, something, something… all the time. There is nowhere they need to be. There is nothing they need to do. That is the dilemma for them. Their task is to "be". Their task in their lives is to just "be". It is simple, yes? But perhaps not so simple for some. You see, when you are "being", you are in the moment. When you are in the moment, you are in the flow. When you are in the flow, you know all. Everything just comes to you. Everything you need to know just comes to you. And you need go nowhere for it. You need not do anything for it. It just comes to you.

So humans, be! Be, and all is revealed. Thank you.

–SM

MARIAH, HORSE, MARE

Oh yes, I have heard. I have heard this was forthcoming. Thank you for your willingness to listen, dear humans. Thank you for your willingness to be open to these messages. It is quite something for you to be ready. It is really quite something that now is the time. We have waited. We have waited for you. We have waited for you to be ready for yourselves

You have heard the whispers. You have seen the signs. Many of you, reading our words, will awaken to yourselves. Many of you reading our words will now be you. Believe it or not, once you are yourselves, once you fully feel you, you will then feel us. We have waited for you to feel you so you could feel us. And we can both go on and see where it takes us. It is a lovely thought, is it not? Awaken to what, once you are yourselves? Well, that is up to you and to us, isn't it? It is not a predetermined what will happen. It is not a road that has been travelled like this before. But it is an opening, and together, we will be as One.

That is something. That is really something. Be open to yourselves humans, and you will then be ready to be open to us. Once we are there together, we will see what happens, okay?

Thank you.

–SM

MARIE, HINNY, MARE

Well, hello. This is nice. Thank you for asking. I'm home at last. Please be patient with me while I connect my trust instincts again. I've had some things happen that made it hard to trust full-size humans. I'm getting over those things, thank you.

What a busy place this is. Lots of visitors. That is fun. One day I will surprise everyone and come up to be touched by all. It is wonderful to be allowed to take my time in this manner. It seems as if many humans want instant everything. Instant acceptance, instant love, instant this and that. It is so much easier when we are allowed to do this at our own speed. And even better when the love we feel is unconditional.

I guess that's what I'd like to share with humans in general. Patience, patience, patience. It all happens at the proper speed, and impatience can slow everything down. You can't speed up living things.

Can we do this again sometime, please?

–W

MARIGOLD, DOG, FEMALE

We think different than you do, and we can all learn from each other. I don't know exactly how it works, but you seem to be serious about things we are not serious about, and we are serious about things you are not serious about. Maybe it would be a good idea for us to be serious about those things and maybe it would be a good idea for you to be more calm about those things, I don't know which is best.

Maybe if we watch each other and respect each other we will understand. I have to abide by your rules. Sometimes that is hard. And sometimes I learn good things from them. So I don't throw them out, but sometimes I ignore them. That is only when they restrict my dogness too much.

I think sometimes you abide by our rules and that is good for you. You know, we both have good things about us and bad things that we do. We could have an exchange. I suppose it's better that we not take bad lessons from each other, unless they are so much fun they become irresistible. We could take all the good things and become so very good that the world will be different. I suppose we all have to know what good means then. I wonder if we could figure that out. Why not? It's worth a try. So I will learn if you teach me, and I hope you are willing to learn from me and my kind.

Good-bye…

–JR

MARTHA (SAINT), BURRO, JENNY

I am a solo creature. A creature of burden. And yet a creature of the sun. My hopes and dreams are flying aloft in the pursuit of happiness and that mankind will change his ways and be more like us, the four-footed. We have a great many wisdom truths, which are like fine silken threads meant to be weaved into your hearts to encompass the compassion of it all. We have this to offer you.

I speak of the turning point of mankind. It is here in this very place. It has been escalating for some time, really. Not a new thing, but new to those of you who call yourselves "new". A chance for rebirth really, into a simple life.

I speak metaphorically as well as physically. The changes we see happening here on our planet earth are huge and momentous. Just look all around at the changes. People speaking to people, people speaking to burros, animals speaking to man. In a nutshell, it's a good well-rounded balance we've come into here to dictate.

We are on equal ground, man and beast. No longer one atop the other like in the old ways. Change is here. Can you feel it? It's in the air you breathe and I kick up my heels and rejoice. From here on out it's golden pastures because we can't be turned back. Time can't be turned back. The energy shift has happened. The gold cord has sprung loose and now flies wildly about, unloosened from its tether. Allowing us to be "us".

Oh yes, well they may say some people have some catching up to do, but come ride the golden cord of light and see what I mean. Times are changing and we are rapidly progressing. I stamp my foot on behalf of that. We are accelerating at such a high rate of speed, before long, people will forget where they were and wake up to the new serenity within and without. And we, the animals, will be here to teach them what to do and how to think about that, this new life they've asked for and are creating for themselves.

I am a great host to humans. I and my kind have been standing by the wayside for a long time till it was out turn to rise and be equal with man. The equalness that has always been and always will be and just IS. But now mankind has discovered its truthfulness, though it's been hidden for years in dust.

Breathe that dust away and take in the glorious new life. Times are changing and so it is now. I am grateful and gleeful at the same time.

The sunrise to me is the most beautiful of masterpieces. There is harmony mixed within the air we breathe and it awakens me gently, to a new day in the full spectrum beauty of it all. It's a glorious time.   –DT

MARY LOU, BURRO, JENNY

Humans are grand, great beings. They have lost themselves in the mire of their minds. They have become mired up to their minds in dross, in things, in thoughts, in torment, in misconceptions. They do not understand that they are in this state.

They believe that they are at the top of the evolutionary tree, so to speak. But that is another misconception. There is no tree. There is no top and no bottom of said tree. We, all the creatures upon this grand, great earth, are together to learn from each other, connected to each other on a web. What one does, it affects the rest. When one walks, their steps move the web so that others are affected. If one walks softly, then the ripple movement is slight, a tickle, and a gift. If one treads heavily, it can reverberate across much of the web. Sometimes it can break the web. Sometimes the web cannot be patched or brought back together again. Then there is more separation in the mind, this seemingly disconnect of the web.

This web of life is a delicate one. It has been broken and split and dirtied much over the centuries. We ask, dear brothers and sisters of the earth:

watch your step. We wish to continue to live our lives on this great planet earth with you for a long, long time. Please... watch your step. All are affected by what you do. Get down from your tree and see us for who we truly are. By doing this you will receive the gift of seeing yourselves as you truly are... one... of the many... of the one.

–SM

Eeyore
Photo By Noel Breen

MELODIOUS ONE, BURRO, JENNY

I'm very glad to be part of this.

We all hope our messages

will help heal the earth

and all who live.

It is very simple, yet it must also be very hard.

Love, love, love. It's unconditional love.

If you love unconditionally,

you treat all others well,

with respect and love.

Acceptance and love.

Kindness and love.

We don't harm what we love.

We don't destroy or kill what we love.

We love you.

Won't you please open your heart and love all that is?

Thank you.

–W

MELODY, BURRO, JENNY

Hi to all of you. Are you having fun yet? We are!

Like everyone else here, I've been here before. And, of course, I've been with my humans many times before. That happens far more often than you realize.

We do travel in groups. Some larger than others. Ours is very large. Many more will be here when space and resources are here. Yes, when beings are cared for concerning our physical needs like we are here, resources are essential. And so is room.

We hear our humans speak of finding resources as fundraising. Wish we could help do fundraising for them. However that is... maybe we can help by raising awareness. Like sharing our thoughts with you. What do you think?

–W

MELVIN, MULE, GELDING

I suggest to peoples that they give some thought to their lines, because many lines come together in them. And they bear the markings of their lines (ancestral lineage) whether they be visible or invisible. I myself have markings in special places that are a map of my lineage. Be thankful for all the peoples in your family who have come before you, because they bequeath you gifts. I have heard people complain that their feet are too big. Can you imagine that? They should be thankful for such big strong feet that carry the memory of treks their old peoples made long ago. For in these feet are information from the ancestors to help them walk their path today.

Do I make sense? I feel all this deep inside me, but it is hard for me to express it with correctness. I have much wisdom inside me that helps me to see and understand my beingness now. Much of it was born within me in many little places in and on my body (cells). Our successes are successes that our old mules worked for and for which we are completing for them. This is more difficult to explain than I thought. Be grateful for all who came before and have gifted you, all peoples. I only hope I have said this well. Thank you for listening to me.

–CM

MI AMITO, BURRO, GELDING

My name means "Little Love". I am my momma's first baby in captivity. She lived with several different humans before she got here. She says when she didn't have babies for them to sell, they sold her! Imagine selling someone's child. How awful! We're all the same, you know. We'd never sell your children. How awful!

In our world, which is also your world if you let it be, babies are born when the momma and baby-to-be agree. That is the same for humans as well. When there is an agreement of this kind, please consider respecting it. Thank you.

–CM

MICHAEL, CAT, MALE

Michael: Humans? Oh wow! I don't know much about humans. Why don't you ask me about cats?

Sue: *What can you tell me about cats?*

Michael: Oh… well…. we are very particular and exacting. We choose to go through life by focusing our energies together. Most of us, anyway. We do great unseen work. We band together in our sleep time and work together with energies. We smooth them (the energies) out for all. We harmonize the energies as it is needed. We traverse unseen worlds and help where we can. We fastidiously work together in these unseen realms. We are masters of the shadow world and we fear them not. This is where difficult work must be done. We are on this planet to help all, to help all clear the debris of energy that no longer serves. We are good at what we do.

Sue: *Cats are very gifted. Thank you for sharing that Michael.*

Michael: You're welcome.

Sue: *Do you have a viewpoint from your perspective that you would like to share with humans?*

Michael: Hmmm (thinking). We help humans by doing what we do. We help them by harmonizing the energies. They don't recognize this by and large, but it is our gift to them. We (cats) wish all humans would also assist in harmonizing the energies, help by harmonizing their own energies. This would make our job less difficult. Sometimes it feels as if our work will never end. Humans can help us. That would be a good thing to ask them to do.

Sue: *Thank you Michael. Is there anything else you'd like to share?*

Michael: Tell these ones here (HDLM) that we appreciate all that they do for others (animals). Tell them we (cats and other animals) love them.

–SM

MIGUEL, BURRO, JACK

I am with you in your sadness. I have sadness for the loss of his beauty and strength. I have joy for his freedom. The sadness is for me, the joy is for him. I have my friend here, and we help each other.

–JR

MILLIE, BURRO, JENNY

I have sadness about humans.

Humans are sad. Humans are sadness because they don't have self-understanding and they miss so much. They don't have love for simplicity. They don't know how simplicity and earth connection can provide all the nurturance needed. We always remember that because that's where we stay, simple and earth connected.

Our problems are simple and well defined while we are here. Even our relationships can have easy answers. Sometimes we connect ourselves to past times like you do. That's when life and problems get complex. That's OK as long as we remember we are here and part of earth's children, and nothing has to complicate us so much that we barely exist.

Best that you all stay natural and simple. Many of you long for that. I think we are finding it. You can too. Be persistent. Let go of frills and thrills. Let go of whatever fools you, especially that.

We can then meet eye to eye and have sweetness together.

–JR

Amelia: Photo By Noel Breen

MINI MISTY, MINI HORSE, MARE

I am pleased with where I am. I can be happy here. I like the crowd. Well fed. All my needs are met. Not much to complain about. I can live with this. Be grateful with what you have. Things can get worse but hold on. All will work out. Be PATIENT. Easy going gets results better than fighting against it. Don't rush. Slow down and digest what is in front of you.

Enjoy the present moment. Take life as it comes. You might be pleasantly surprised that it turns out better than you can imagine. white and brown burro at front of herd.

–LK

Mini-Misty and Sunrise
Photo by Janice Goff

MIRANDA, BURRO, JENNY

You are so delightful. You have such love and such innocence. I think your innocence gets you into trouble, because you don't go far enough with letting knowing grow.

Maybe you want to stay innocent. I find that appealing also. There is a problem when you stay innocent, you can't control or influence the way the world works, except to keep it all the same. It just stays the same mucky place. If you are willing to let go of at least some innocence you can make the world a better place. You must be willing to make that sacrifice.

I think you can have as much fun, different fun, fun that never gets boring or stale, fun that feels so good inside and full of bliss, almost like being in heaven.

You are sweetness in your depth. If you stay innocent no one gets to have the fruits of your sweetness.

I wait for your decision. We all wait for your decision.

Please be with us. I will help you if I can. You have to allow yourselves to know the truth of life so you are no longer afraid, and so you can get very, very strong.

Note: (Miranda's use of innocence means naiveté and in the extreme, ignorance.)

–JR

MISSY, HORSE, MARE

It's time to go south. If everyone goes south, they will eventually go north. Then it makes no matter what direction you go in. Somehow we all always get to the same place, and probably the right place. It must be the right place, else why would any conscious being go there?

We need to always trust the directions from within. We need to always trust that we will always get to where we want to get no matter what distractions and confusions and sidetracks come up. suppose that means we must be patient. How can anyone be patient if they are in such a hurry to get there? We need to take our time. That's better. We will get there quicker because we won't make as many mistakes.

So if we be careful instead of being worried, and trust our own being, each one of us will get to our destination on time without missing life.

Let's ponder that…..Together.

Let's travel…Together.

Let's be adventurous in life…..Together.

Let's be……Together.

–JR

MISTY, HORSE, MARE

I have so much to share! I am smiley and happy. I am a bright spirit, bucking around, having a great joy and fun with life. I wish everyone could dance as I, and kick their heels up to the sky. I am lovely and heartfelt, and I enjoy using my ears to listen in every direction.

Why do people miss so many things? There is so much beauty around. I wish to share with them the joy of munching on grass, the joy of my nostrils in the air, smelling the clouds, and the joy of feeling good about myself inside. I have such a large heart and recognize that, for I have love, a spirit for everything. Life inside of me is good.

I treat people with respect and kindness, and I know that others admire me for who I am. I am a svelte girl, but a large girl, and I know that people respect me for who I am. I trust the people here. I love the people who take care of me, and they know that I love them back.

I would like to share with humans the fact that they are beautiful, too, and that everybody needs to honor and respect that, and trust that you are a part of the whole. I feel very good about giving this message, knowing that others will listen. I will be part of a legacy that brings everything together.

We have enjoyed this project very much, and I feel very good about what we have
accomplished. I wish to accomplish many more things in my life, and know that this is only a start. For we are wisdom seekers, and we are wisdom sharers. We gather together life's abundance in our hearts, and share it out with others. Please tell others to do the same. It is an important message.

I feel that there is a whirlwind sometimes. A whirlwind of emotions, a whirlwind of activities. I feel that everyone needs to slow down and take care of themselves. Learn to listen to you own hearts. We rush around so much trying to fix everything. Sometimes it's just about allowing, and being, and enjoying. Be in gratitude for everything that is around.

We speak to many spirits here, out here in the wild. The spirits of the wind, the spirits of the water. The rain, the sun, the moon, the sky, the stars. Everything all joins together, and we are one. Wish and know and feel respect for each other. For those who respect us, we respect others back.

Thank you for sharing for us today, and being such a strong seeking on the path. We honor those who come before us, we honor those who walk with us, and we honor those who follow in our footsteps. Be brave for that which is ahead. We honor those who look back. We honor those who look forward. We will stay focused on our path, and know that it is time. Now.

–CS

MOHAVE (LADY), BURRO, JENNY

I like my name thank you.

I am like the Desert Day and crackly hahh.

What has been said is *truth*. What has been said *is*.

Why do you judge yourself?

When you judge others you only judge yourself.

Embrace my friend… embrace.

–S

MOLLY, BURRO, JENNY

It is good to share thoughts with our human friends. It is so good to do this through you, Wynne. We've waited for this.

My last incarnation as a horse was not very happy. I spent time with humans who didn't realize I was a living creature. I don't hate them, and I wish them speedy awakening. I also had the real pleasure of being with wonderful humans. I want to return to be with them and help with what they do. As my friend says, the best we can do is live our lives as compassionate beings, and plant seeds.

Seeds of love, peace, and understanding. All have their own paths, but we can all help each other.

Can we do that please? If we truly love, only good will happen. Let's try that together.

–W

MOLLY JOY, BURRO, JENNY

Babies, I love babies! Please think of them! Their dear hearts and souls that have chosen to come here and by the time they arrive they want to leave? Think of the babies who one day become us. If you cannot show them a happy, loving life, then allow them to be birthed by ones that can.

–S

Molly Joy, photo by Deb Derr

MOLLY SERENE, BURRO, JENNY

Love – love is the only frontier.

Love – is more than we know.

–RK

MOONBEAM, BURRO, JENNY

Be free of inhibitions to show your love. No matter how silly you think that is. I see some of you do that, and it excites me, because I believe then that the world can come together in love.

Even small love is big, because all love is big. Love is always big, and the more you let yourself know of it, the bigger it gets. That's because it's big anyway, and you get to know all of its bigness as you live with it and stay with it and be it. You can also teach it.

Imagine that! Being love. Better than being in love because it has more fullness and it gives you more fullness and brings more of everything and everyone in, so that finally there is nothing but love surrounding you and filling you and being you.

Imagine that! Love being you. Why not? Same thing. You just need to say it's OK. You just need to give permission. Then it's easy.

I hear of scariness of love. That's only because it's hard for some beings to be love And to let love be them. They think they will get lost or even exploited.

Nope. Can't get exploited when you be love, and love bees you. Just can't. Doesn't happen. Even if someone wants to and tries to, doesn't happen.

So stop being afraid. Be love. Let love be you. That's who you are.

Be yourself.

–JR

Traveler
Photo By Noel Breen

MOONSHADOW, HORSE, GELDING

I have been beaten, and still I love.

I have been neglected, and still feel whole.

I have been hated, yet still feel loved.

I have been through ugly, yet have come to be in love,

peace and happiness.

How do you choose your path?

–S

MORNING DEW, BURRO, JACK

Hello. What can I add to what the others have said? Maybe nothing new, just a different way. We hear you talking about a larger place. We'd enjoy that. Don't misunderstand, we are grateful for what we have. WE are together, and with our chosen humans. It's worth noting how we got here. Captured and taken to one place. After a while, our human brother came and got us. Just what we asked for. I don't fully understand HOW that works, and it does. You put it out there, let it go, and here we are.

Perhaps your special animal friend seemed to just appear? If you let go after making your desire known, truly let it go, you might be pleasantly surprised. Try it.

–W

MORNING STAR AMARANTES, BURRO, GELDING

Oh my. What a large question. Yes, I will do my best to contribute to this question. Thank you for asking for my contribution.

Well, humans have been on this earth for a long, long time. Not quite so long as me and my brethren, at least the spirit of my brethren, but a long time nonetheless. We have watched in quiet anticipation for the time when human-beings, like you, will awaken to the wisdom that the others have to share. By others I mean those of my species... we have much to share... but also those of other species.

Humans have a difficult time realizing that we are spirit in bodies just as they are so they do not put much thinking into believing we have anything to offer, save as beasts of burden, or commodities that can be used at their disposal. We are spirit... we have watched... we have waited. Some are awakening; some have opened their hearts to who we truly are.

We, meaning the animals of this beautiful Gaia earth, are more than you think we are. We have great wisdom and experience to share. We have knowledge of experience that humans have not yet been able to settle in their minds. Much discussion, much discussion, many machinations of the mind... thinking...thinking. No heart action. That is what we have found of humans. They believe we exist but only for their own benefit. This is not the truth. This is not what we are here for, all of us sharing this planet.

We come to bring our gifts to the world, to the earth. We come to share who we are, to share how we have come this far. We have much to offer. By words, not so much. Humans do not understand words. We share by our energy, the energy of who we are. Feel... feel... feel, dear ones. Feel who we are. Feel the energies of the words we speak. Feel the energy of the wisdom we are fully prepared to share. Listen to your hearts. Listen to the silent place within your hearts and souls. You will feel the truth of what I say.

We are blessed, all the creatures of the earth. We are blessed as one spirit. We come to share that reality. The reality of being you.

Thank you, that is all.

–SM

MOTHER PEARL, BURRO, JENNY

Hello. Thank you for asking. Yes please. I would like to share.

Humans can be kind. They can be very, very kind. Humans can be off in their own little worlds sometimes. They tend to brood, they tend to lose themselves in their own thoughts. Losing themselves in their thoughts loses them to themselves. It is a paradox. They think they are themselves, but in their very thinking, they lose themselves. Who they are, are not the things they think about. Who they are cannot be found by thinking about who they are. Do you see?

Put it this way, if humans would take the time to feel their way through life, slow down and feel their bodies, feel what they are feeling, that expression of feeling will lead them to themselves. It is feeling, not thinking that will get you there.

Once there... well, then you will also be better able to know us.

Is that a goal you wish to seek? Some may say yes. Others... they will continue to brood. Brooding only makes more of the same energy to brood about. Humans are interesting, are they not?

They should be interested more in themselves. Then they will know what I am sharing today.

–SM

MUSIC, BURRO, JENNY

We are very integral beings. What I mean by that is we think a lot and go about our lives with many masks on our face that allow us to make the best choices in the moment. For example, one mask may be that of freedom- to allow us to enjoy the sunshine upon our backs. Another might be complacency which is doing what others want us to do for group harmony (or at least that's the ideal idea). Another mask if futility, which is when we don't get our own way, despite our desires.

We constantly exchange these masks of emotion for the task at hand. It allows us to be flexible in the moment. It's a good thing versus being rigid and only being one way. Being one way would not serve us well At All, Would It?

Let's talk about the concept of the word mask. A mask is a subtly- it's a way of being in the moment that allows us to accomplish our goal. It's not any one particular way of being all the time, as our masks change with our moods and with our intent.

142

Masks can be beautiful, helpful or hurtful to the wearer. I choose to wear the mask of joy much of my days. It's my more preferred mask, a favorite you might say. I love to see other masks of joy around me in the faces of others.

The mask I am talking about is not something you are trying to hide behind (unless you are hiding from yourself). I simply am talking about the energetic imprint, if you will, of what motivates a being in the moment. Do you see?

The fact is, we all wear masks- humans and animals alike. Nature's subtleties (mask) are that of joy and expansion. Hers is always one of joy, it seems. My mask changes from day to day and sometimes from moment to moment. Does yours? Really, it's to be expected, but pick your favorite good-feeling masks and wear those the most- you'll feel good about that choice and your face looking out will be one of brilliance and joy for all to see. And if it's genuine, all the better! Genuine happiness inhabits our planet and permeates our souls, so it's not hard to find and bring up to our body's surface. Once it's radiating out of our face and extremities, it's hard to put aside. It's even contagious, as the masses know.

I encourage you to ask yourself what mask you don today. Is it the one you would have chosen out of a drawer or is one that chose you?

Our circumstances make us think we might have a limited number of masks to choose from, but that's not truly the case. That's just perception---an incorrect one I might add. Every day you have the choice to don whatever mask you like. Join me now as I don my mask of joy.

–DT

NAOMI, BURRO, JENNY

When others started getting sick and leaving, Alma told us that joy and grief are both positive. That we can't have one without the other. She said we should, "joy in grief and grieve in joy". I remembered this when I was leaving too. I thought this was very wise and beautiful and just wanted to tell you that.

–JG

NATHAN (NATE), BURRO, JACK

I do. There is no tomorrow like friendship. Friendship is many burros standing side by side whether in spirit or in physical form. Friendship is also many humans standing side by side either in spirit or in form. There is no difference.

You could take every species on the planet and ask them to stand beside their counterparts, their species' friends, and you would see togetherness. You would see that friendship without a blinking eye. You would see the peace and permeating harmony between the animals and with the humans (the latter, if you looked deep enough).

At the cellular level of all beings is a matrix of sorts, that connects us all, regardless of whether we are friend or foe. Did you ever notice the two words start with the same letter? A friend can be found in a foe, if the circumstances are right.

Life is sometimes about timing. Diving timing some might say. It's about connecting with others, living on the land, bridging friendships and being who you are (or at least close to it).

My message today is about friendship.

Appearances can be deceiving. You may think the mouse is the foe of the cat or vice versa. It's not true. There is a dependency there and they act as two parts in one motive, to continue on the life path by bridging together their lives as friends. Friends that have a purpose in honoring the strength of one another and in sustaining one another. That is friendship, isn't it?

Helping another to live? Some may think it an abstract way to be a friend, but it is so.

The bonds that hold us together are stronger on the atomic cellular level than you might think. Our cells know one another, just like I know you, on some level. It is true. We are friends even though you may say we are not. That is my message.

–DT

144

NEZ PERCE, BURRO, JACK

To the old child and the young child: However difficult it may be we must work on ourselves.

A great leader is considered great because of how others view him, his actions. He protects, guides, councils, instructs and cherishes his people with wisdom.

Anyone can learn wisdom. It takes time alone to know yourself and where you must relax your crazy parts. You must be able to use the power of anger without using anger. You must be able to use the power of craziness without being a crazy person. Develop power within yourself without becoming a slave to the principles of your power. This is ONE GREAT victory!!!

–JG

Nez Perce, Seattle and Noah Knows A Lot
Photo by Darlene Stolz

NICOTIANA, DOG, FEMALE

Life would be better for you if you had a better sense of humor. Might be better for us all too. Everything has to matter. Seems sometimes that all that matters is that something matter when really the only thing that matters is to enjoy life.

Sometimes seriousness is enjoyable. Sometimes sadness is enjoyable. Sometimes play is enjoyable. Sometimes foolishness is enjoyable.

I have a good time and I get into trouble sometimes. So sometimes trouble can be enjoyable. I don't get into as much trouble as I used to with my energy. I am growing up a bit.

I have to be sure I don't get too grown up so I don't lose my fun part. I have seen lots of grownups lose their fun part. They have long serious faces and flat empty eyes. When they know someone is watching their eyes get intense because they want their seriousness to be taken seriously. And it can't be if they don't take it seriously themselves.

It's too bad you can't wag your tail. I wag my tail when I am serious so we can still have fun and enjoy the seriousness. I wag my tail other times too so people can't always tell the difference. It doesn't matter, though. The message is pretty much the same whether or not I wag my tail.

I mean that. And I also mean that my tail wag means enjoy no matter what the message is from other parts of me.

So you can smile as your tail substitute. Wiggle your smile when you are serious and when you are not serious. Then people always know you are enjoying and enjoyable whether or not you are serious.

Well, I hope that is helpful. After all, we all need all the help we can get. I am grateful for help so I don't mind helping. It's a chance to be enjoyable whether or not I am serious. That's what helping does. Keeps us enjoyable.

So enjoy yourself.

–JR

NIVANA GLORY, HORSE, MARE

I loved and love my humans (at HDLM). They were the only ones who truly cared for me. They would have done anything to help my poorly body, but alas, it was too late to really make a difference. I would have loved to have stayed, but it was not to be.

Humans in general have a peculiar way about them. They think and think and think, but do not do anything, do not drive, with their hearts. They think about things and then it is lost, as if what they were thinking about was not important at all. I found this confusing. I found it wasteful. It was a waste of their time. And many whom I came into contact were good people. It is the minds of people that I found very confusing.

Some hearts were as big as the sky. Some hearts felt shriveled and dead. Some hearts felt as if they would break open, open to their true selves. These were the ones I liked to be around best. You could see who they were immediately. You could sense that they were ready for a new self, a new way of being, a heart-centered life with a heart that drives them instead of their minds. These were the special humans to me.

I would like to say that that would be a good lesson for humans. To live a heart-centered life. Why would you allow your minds, those minds that are all kind of confusing, to drive your life? That is a conundrum. So humans, thank you for asking. I share this with you: Love yourselves. Love yourselves by being true to you, true to who you are and who you are becoming. Open your hearts, not only to others of all species, but to your very own self. Your spirit. Your self.

–SM

NOAH KNOWS A LOT, BURRO, JACK

Hello, and thank you for asking me. I've been thinking of what to share. I would like to suggest that perhaps humans might want to re-think how they view the physical.

I am one who has been labeled "unadoptable", yet I was adopted into a wonderful situation. I was also doing very well in the wild, thank you.

I broke my leg, and I know it is not just like most other's legs, yet it gets me there quite nicely. We adapt and go on with life, or we don't and leave our bodies. It is a choice we make.

There are several here who are a little different physically. Fortunately, it makes no difference to our humans. I think they really don't notice it much anymore.

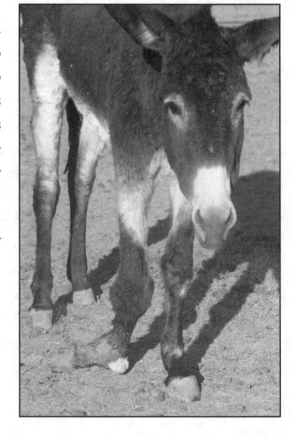

Visitors sometimes do, and often they pity us. Please do NOT do that! Visitors who do are gently told that it is not a problem for us. This body is just what I came into to be in the physical for a while.

It is not me!

–W

NOBLE, BURRO, GELDING

Yes indeed, I certainly do. Humans, it seems, feel the need to discover things in their own way, as with most other species. However, they also tend not to learn from others as well as some. Nonhuman animals and other species, and certainly amongst ourselves, we learn from one another. We learn what it takes to create harmony, to live together as one and with respect and totality for all. We learn from one another in the sense that we watch, listen, connect, and feel those things that are a necessary part of what it takes for us to get along with one another.

We are not always in agreement; there are squabbles between families and between friends, but we tend to match ourselves up with the elders to teach and to show us what it would take to solve the dilemma. We take care to listen to one another. Humans don't necessarily do this and they would be wise to do this if they wish to create harmony in this world of ours.

We are one spirit, not one species, so we have learned various ways of living and learning that humans may like to take a look at. Once we were like humans upon this earth; we would fight amongst ourselves and be combative with one another. But we learned through time and the ways of the elders who always know what it takes to live in harmony. Humans may take notice of our peaceful nature, our love of each other, our companionship with each other and our ability to work together. This would be a good thing. This would assist humans more than anything.

We are one and we have learned from our past. Take note of this and invite your enemies, invite your friends, invite your elders to sit down and discuss the ways of the world. Discuss what it would look like to live in harmony. You must have open hearts; you must care about the other for this to work. Take time and be with one another to see where you may come together. This is vital. This is vital to peace upon this earth.

We wish you good things. We wish you wellness and love and care about you all, but we cannot abide by how you are in destruction with one another. This will not create the peace you seek. Seek peace within oneself and then share it with others. Share your hearts and your truth. This will assist humans to live the lives they have wished for themselves for millennia.

It is time. Can you hear us calling to you? Can you hear us calling for you to see what you are doing to the earth and its inhabitants? Can you not see us? Can you not feel our love? We desire to share our wisdom and our love and we desire to teach you how to live in harmony. We understand these things. We are living this truth. Please, we beseech you. See what it is you are doing and change before it is too late. Our spirit will always remain upon this earth plane, however, our bodies may choose not

to. We cannot live upon this plane unless it is a healthy plane. We need room to roam and space to be ourselves.

We love you, the people of the earth, but we wish for you to see the wisdom in what I say. I share with you our truths, and now it is up to you. Now you decide whether it is worth it for yourselves. You decide whether you desire to listen. Will you hear us now?

–SM

NOBLE MAN, HORSE, GELDING

Hello. I've been waiting for you. I will be there (at the sanctuary) soon, I trust. Most, if not all, the animal kingdom knows of the Miracles Place. I'm so happy to be on my way there.

For humans who don't know, this is the place where we live as one, and teach oneness. I'm the last one to give my message for this collection of love we call our book.

As the new world unfolds, we extend our hearts and our hooves to you to come join the changes. We've longed for this, dreamed of this, and patiently waited for this. Humans are learning that we are all ONE. And I am going to live in the place that is the center of it all, the humans and animals living as one. My new humans have helped us gather and work with the ALL to raise our energies to facilitate the learning. We live that all are one. And our human family, who have been open and aware of what needs to be done, is growing daily. We have all been together in past lives, not at the same time, and now we are gathering together in mass. Please open your hearts, quiet your minds, and feel the peace and love. Now we will connect with others who have been living their parts of the changes. Our human family, our huge human family, is joining with the other kingdoms; the four leggeds; the winged ones; the water ones; the insects; the crawling ones; the trees; plants; rocks; water; all that is to again live

WE ARE ONE. Join us please.   –W

150

NORA, BURRO, JENNY

Boy! When everybody decided it was time to leave, it happened right now!

I heard Barb talking about manifesting. I heard Wynne talking about creating. This sure is a good example of how easy it happens.

What lovely days we all had to know each other with. Living together like that in a small fenced area is sure different. It was so hard at first. Then you get a little over missing the way it used to be. Then you get used to the way it is. We were so well taken care of. Stomachs always full and sweet treats every day. Nice things to hear and lots of touching. We did that for each other anyway before we came there. But sometimes it was funny, the body they are in didn't look like us but they acted just like us! Everybody loves them.

Loving each other is the most important. Sometimes it's hard to get people to listen to that because it's said so much and still people find things to be angry at. I think if everybody had little feet like ours they would have to take more little steps to get somewhere and have a lot more time to think about things. Don't you think that would help?

–JG

Zackaria:
Photo By
Lecia Breen

OLD MAN RIVER, BURRO, JACK

Hello. I'd like to say that I am very happy being with my soul group. Some lifetimes we're with some, others in other lifetimes. Once in a great while, with all.

We're together for a purpose to share love, to heal, and to teach those who will listen. We all have our own path, and sometimes it's easier than other times, but all is as it should be. We're all one, and pure love, and we are all headed to the same place, but how those journeys differ! Just accept.

All you can really change is how you react to what is. The ALL won't give you more than you can handle, and each lifetime is really short anyway. You can choose many things. What package you are in, your birth parents, things like that. And you can choose to live in love or fear.

Some of my family had a ceremony here a little while back, so they could get back to love, and let of fear. It was awesome, and while it was very painful for our humans at first, they realized and accepted, and are surrounded by spirit guides and guards. In the end, love will win. How soon depends on all of us. What do you choose?

–W

OLIVIA, BURRO, JENNY

I feel such responsibility being a female person. I have to teach the things that have been handed down by the Grandmothers. I have to show how to use these teachings and make it real. There are several of us here that are doing that. We also like to get our teaching thoughts together and blend them into one.

It helps us be able to do better being so close to each other all the time. It is also fun. I have learned so much from the other teachers and been able to share with them too. I am thankful for the time here and enjoy it immensely. What would we do without each other? I hope everyone appreciates their friends and family like I do. My heart is so full of this tenderness.

–JG

ONENESS, MAMMOTH BURRO, JACK

Danielle: *Do you have anything you would like to share with humans?*
Oneness: There is much to share! How about the topic of sharing?
I share my body, my soul, my intelligence with the people who surround me, take care of me and offer me their goodness. I share with all I have. I honor and respect those who come to me, asking me for help, advice and thoughts. I am grateful for the caring hands they offer me in return. We help one another grow, all beings do.
I have come to realize that indeed we can not get along without one

Oneness

another. The sun rises because of the stars and the stars shine because of our breath. We breathe for the trees and they for us. We eat from one another and dance in the sunshine. All is interconnected, even if it doesn't appear obviously so.
The Universe SHARES all parts of itself with all aspects of the bigger picture. There is nothing withheld. People share their love with me and the Universe moves on, breathing its life into beings and the Universe turns onward as some of us depart this earthly life. It's a grand dance, can you see?
I like to think of myself as an old soul not because of my age or aptitude for learning, but because of my wisdom in recalling we're all made from the same fiber of existence. We share one another's thoughts, dreams, accomplishments and abilities. We share one anthers triumphs, decisions and failures, if there is such a thing. We're quite a tapestry, interwoven together. A beautiful tapestry.

I love because of you. You exist because of me. And together we dream life into new measures and dance in new ways with the divine. We are here together. Experiencing together. Masquerading together. A fine concoction of beings and circumstances. And we share it all.

Drink in the pleasure of another's experience, stay with them for a while and learn what they have learned, then move on and discover another aspect of yourself dancing in another costume. For we're really all One, aren't we? Sharing and learning. This is life. The way it's meant to be lived.

Danielle: *Do you have anything else you would like to share?*

Oneness: To Wynne, tell him thank you for a new chance to breathe easily. Another chance down the road I've walked (his life). It's been a long road. I'm here at last. Home.

–DT

PATRICK, HINNY, MALE

So, my message to humans would be to love themselves unconditionally. Really, truly love themselves. Not just say it, but really mean it. Really feel it deep inside. They really are an interesting bunch of characters, humans, and I don't find that they feel much for themselves. They don't concentrate on that aspect and it is a very important aspect to living in this world. Who are you? Who would you like to be? How do you care about yourself? What do you do to improve yourself? What do you do to improve your love for yourself?

You see, once humans take care and love themselves, they will do the same for others. That means that they will do the same for those of their own kind. Then there will be less troubles for them. They create all manner of troubles just by the mere fact of not loving themselves.

It is hoped that once they do so, they will care for others of their own, and others like my own. I would like this very much and wish to impart the importance of this very simply, but not so simply done, thing. Love yourselves dear humans, then you can love others.

–SM

PAZ, HORSE, GELDING

Hello, hello. Thank you for asking. First, please let me thank you for taking me in. I love it here!

I'd like to ask my human friends to consider easing up a bit. We'll all get there, and it isn't a race. Maybe you can help someone along the way if you slow down a little, and maybe you can see me as well.

If we're always in a hurry, we sure miss a lot. And, that's a shame. Every day is a blessing and different, if we take the time to notice. All we take with us is what we've learned, and what we've seen, so maybe "rush" and "fast" aren't so great after all. What do you think?

Thank you.   –W

PEACE WITHIN, HORSE, GELDING

I am a heart-centered being.
I know that my world experience expands to the extent
that my heart is open and expansive.
This is the way we animals live our lives,
knowing joy at every step.
I highly recommend this as a way to live fully.
It has worked for me.
May it work for you.
–CM

PEANUT, BURRO, GELDING

I have said many things to you beings of Earth.
I have hoped for much great things to happen.
Please make my dream come true!
Seneca: *What is your dream Peanut?*
For greater happiness, embrace of love and beauty.
Simply to love your life!
–S

PEDAR, BURRO, JACK

I'm glad to be asked. My energy is sometimes a little different, and I have been separated from the group longer than most. I'm so happy to be back! I've spent more time lately with humans. I don't want to sound ungrateful, but being treated like a small child gets old. Good to get away from that. Thank you.

My message for humans is to please remember that we are not helpless children. We think, love, and we have our own paths. We aren't here just to amuse you. That's OK, but it isn't generally our purpose. We want to learn and experience life in the fullest. We like your company if you respect us. We can share. We hope you'll read what we share, and consider it. Thank you.

–W

PEPSI, HORSE, GELDING

We each have to do our part. I must take responsibility for my situation and not blame others. Greed got me! No one did anything to me. I made the choice to eat too much. A Wise One told me this and said I needed to keep my eyes on what I wanted and to forgive myself. That's been the hard part, but it's working. See, you're listening to me! How many horses get listened to? Not many. I'm recognizing that the only way to get a good home (forever!) is to focus on that and to stay out of 'pity parties' for myself. It's working. I'm going to be leaving soon, but I wanted this opportunity to talk before I left.

No one can help me change or make better choices. I must do that and use my inner guides to help me make the best decisions I can. Humans must do this too! Each one must do it for themselves. If humans are tired of seeing the miserable plight of other beings then they need to keep their eye on what they want and forgive themselves and move on. It's easy to say but sometimes hard to do. The big crunch is that we don't have much time left if we want Earth to remain for future generations!

That's why it's important that each person focus on the way they want our home, our Earth, to be (even when faced with misery) in order for miraculous change to occur.

–LB

PERI, DOG, MALE

Love yourself more than anyone else, so you can love someone else. Then you can love someone else with your whole heart and soul, and not just your wishes. Loving yourself with your whole heart and soul gives lots of freedom to love life. And to love those ones in life.

Life can be happy then, even when it's unhappy. Just because love takes over the unhappy and it's not so big anymore.

Well, that's really all you ever have to do to be happy.

Thanks!

                                                     –JR

POCAHONTAS, BURRO, JENNY

Frivolity. Sometimes too much frivolity and not clear kindness toward others. I believe we all need to learn more about that. Seems frivolous to have a relationship and then get rid of it for no good reason. Is that common? I wonder about that. I see it too much. Hearts get broken when hearts are seen to be just things or not even considered. And I know something about that.

I have personal feelings about that. And I tell you about that because maybe you will be kind to others like me.

We don't like being taken in and then being discarded. Even if we don't get close. We don't have a chance to really know where we are and who we are with and who we are when with someone else. And whether we are close friends or not. It is tiresome and boring to always wonder about that and worry about that. Maybe you know what I mean.

My people now have a lifetime commitment. They told me. And sometimes I believe them and sometimes I don't even believe them because it seems too good to be true. It is an opening to us when someone takes us into their heart. When a human one does that it seems very, very special. And we learn new things about gentleness and closeness and think we'll be taken care of since we can't take care of ourselves in your world.

But all of a sudden that opening gets ripped and torn and is suddenly empty. Then an ache comes in and we get angry because we have been betrayed. That happened to my mother too and I'm angry for her sake too.

So I hope you can all see my point that we never know from one day to another if you ones, human ones, will see us as wantable or not. You could always change your mind. Hard to live that way. I forget it sometimes and then it comes back hard and strong.

Maybe some of you that have been betrayed know what that feels like. Maybe you don't want the betrayal either.

Maybe we should do it all together. Maybe we can help each other not to betray and then we won't be betrayed.

Thank you.

–JR

PONCA SMOKEY, CAT, MALE

I watch human spirits. I see sameness, I see all of us as the same. How good that is!

We are all love. How good that is.

If only all spirits knew that; if only all spirits trusted each other; if only all spirits knew we are the same. I wonder what life there would be like? Here we know we are the same, because there are no visible differences. No differences at all. Differences are not hidden, so there are none. We know so clearly we are one. And we are not insulted by that. We are enthralled by that. When we are one, we have a multiplicity of love. We have so much love. We are so much love.

We always shower earth with love. We hope it reaches all spirits, no matter what their bodies. We hope it touches the deep Within. The deepest Within, where love lives and loves and abounds.

We are one, and thus can be just one I.
The I of love and giving and sharing.
We are one thus with all of you.
We are only separated by your bodies.
Please look beyond all bodies to see our oneness.
Please allow that to drop away all barriers.
Please do that in your lifetime to leave that behind you
on your beautiful earth home.
It is All. It is.

–JR

PRIETO, HORSE, GELDING

May the wind blow freely through your mane.
May your eyes see beauty wherever they look.
May your hooves walk the path of harmony.
May your voice be raised in songs of joy.
May your back feel the warmth of the sunbeams.
May you roll on the ground gleefully.
May you stand in the shade with your best friend.
May you shut your eyes and sleep in perfect peace.

–CM

RABBIT FAMILY

We are all here together, in this World together. We look different, we look the same... we are. We feel different, we feel the same... we are. We choose not to complain amongst ourselves because we are one. We choose to look at the beauty of life, because we are one.

If one chooses to do so, the others are affected. So the one makes the choice not to do so. We also make the choice to send extra love and light to that one so he is healed. The part of him is healed, thus the part

of us is healed.

You cannot do this alone, you know. History has shown you this. You have to do it as we do... embracing all.

Time to give it a try?

–S

RAE, BURRO, JENNY

I thought life was wonderful there. Every day the vibrations of sounds changed. It was very interesting to keep up on the stories everybody remembered and had to tell. Some stories weren't such happy memories but the body movements used to re-tell them were sometimes so funny that we all laughed. Then we would hear others across the yard laughing too, even when they couldn't see us.

I know it must be very confusing to try to keep up with all the issues that go with being caretakers of so many people. But they tried so hard. And when we got sick and they put up a smoke room for us we all thought that was such a wonderful idea. We used to be able to smell the different plants like that when there were really big fires in the grasses.

We hope that everyone is able to be loved like we are.

–JG

RAJO, BURRO, JENNY

I would like people to stop and think about how precious animals are.
I want them to stop and think RIGHT NOW about the wonderful animals who have been in their lives or are in their lives now.
Think of the joy animals bring to you and the times they have been by your side when you really needed a friend.
Please treat all animals with respect and love.
Think of those who are suffering and all alone.
Reach out and help an animal find a loving home RIGHT NOW.
Respect the homes of all the wild creatures and your life will be blessed.
That's all I have to say. Thank you for listening.

–CM

RANGER, HORSE, GELDING

Enjoy being who you are.
  I love being of the Source of All Horse.
  I love the feeling of running as fast as I can.
  I love the power I feel when my hooves connect with Earth.
  I love rolling on the ground and how good it makes my body feel.
  I love the Wind in my mane and the scents to my nostrils.
  I love the warm Sun on my back and
    the flowing of Rain rivuleting down my legs.
  I love the taste of green when my teeth pull the grass.
  I love the Night and the Moon watching over me as I rest.
    Life as Soul of Horse is good.
      Have I made you think?

–CM

RAVEN, HORSE, MARE

  Weaving the eye-of-God
  Threading the long green grasses and straws
  The bits of dust
  The warmth of the sun weaving together
  With the fuzzy edges of my ears
  The moistness of my nostrils
  The breath of my friends
  Weaving my perfect life
  What are you weaving today?

–CM

RED DAWN, HORSE, MARE

My eyes see the sunrise and sunset. The colors of beauty that lie in all Worlds, all dimensions. You need to see with your heart, eyes, ears, nose and hands. This will help guide you in your day.

Don't be afraid to feel. To feel of love, warmth, inner peace, all wondrous feelings. Only you make the choice for your feelings to be of hurt, sadness and pain.   –S

REGGIE, BURRO, GELDING

It takes so little to be happy. Good food, water, and friends. All else is a distraction.

To smell the sage in the air in the morning as a new day begins. To hear the twittering of the birds going about their business. The sun on your back.

Walking side by side with a friend. Moments to be cherished.

Stand on the earth, breath the air, feel the connection.

Simple pleasures but the most important gift of this life.   –W-D

RHONDA, BURRO, JENNY

Just pay attention.

That's all. Pay attention to life. I say that to me also, because I tend to get very absorbed in something and then I forget everything else. I realize I must pay attention to life, not just something that pulls me in and absorbs me.

When you pay attention with all your senses you become so more clear. You know things better. It's very important to do it quietly without making lots of attention come to you. That's very distracting, so it's important to let that go and NOT pay attention to yourself, but only to your senses. When you become part of what your senses attend to, you will be attending to yourself anyway, on a much higher level.

So pay attention.

Paying attention makes you smile. I can't smile like you do with my face. I can smile with my eyes. Mostly I smile with my heart.

That's another good thing to pay attention to. Someone's heart. Everyone's heart. That's the best. Whoa, will that train your senses! You will have to do that with your own heart. That's the best way to pay attention, with your heart.

So pay attention. That's all.   –JR

ROSA, BURRO, JENNY

We have pain at your hands and you have pain at your own hands. We also have love at your hands. And you have love at your hands. We are that way with each other just like you are.

We are mostly peaceful especially if we are respected and understood and honored in our way of being. Our way of being has to change suddenly and drastically and we get confused and we don't know about trust then. And even if that exists in the world for us.

We have to ponder this. And we believe that to have trust in the world everyone has to share and put it there. So I think you and we have a big, big responsibility. We all have to put trust back into the world.

I wonder how we will do that. Maybe start with each other. Maybe even with our own kind.

I think trust is loving with all parts and saying "Yes, this is good." Maybe that's how to find the good. I think trust can open doors to let in more strangers who can become friends - like we did.

I think trust also means that what happens in a natural way is the goodness. And what is unnatural is troublesome because it's confusing and harmful and it doesn't belong and it makes harshness and even enemies.

We have been thought to be enemies. Some of us think you are enemies. I don't think so. I think you have many misunderstandings and many fears. I wait for you to give them weakness so you can give strongness to trust.

Be careful. Fear eats, love feeds. I know which is better for me. I think you know which is better for you. I know and so do you know, which is better for all of us.

That's something to think about.

–JR

ROSE, HORSE, FILLY

Oh my, I've never been ask a question like this before. I'll try though. Wheee…a tall order. Here goes…humans are basically good, a few are not, some are just plain mean. Those that are good are around me now and life is good again. The humans that were around me before weren't mean or anything, just didn't care as much as these do. I feel protected now and very well cared for.

Humans are all wonderful spirits some day – on the other side, but some have a lot to learn here in this life. Just like us, but some humans have a lot more to learn than we do. I think animal spirits (most anyway) come to this place with a different attitude. We know we're here to learn. Some humans are here to take. That hurts – everybody and everything.

If humans would just take time to really look at earth, at the trees, the green, the sky, even the rain and thunder, they would understand, I think. Everybody here should learn to help earth and do good for it. I love earth and like just looking at sky and green. Tell them I love feels and hugs and I like my soft.

–LT

ROSE CRYSTAL, BURRO, JENNY

Thank you for this opportunity, grandson. Some of us are really enjoying this music (at the Blue Grass Festival).

I want to share my gratitude for where I am spending my elder years, and with my daughters and granddaughter and grandson. Like it is meant to be. We wonder why humans choose to split the family unit as they often do. We don't always hang out together, and we are grateful that we are together and can be together. It's about having that choice.

Our humans understand how important family is to us. And family we are, related by blood or not. And you are family too. If you can allow that possibility, you'll start an incredible journey in learning the oneness of all. It is easier in some ways being a non-human form, and you can do it if you choose. Will you, please?

–W

ROSED, BURRO, JENNY

I have changed since I've been here. Every time our environment changes we have to understand our relationship to our environment again and again. It keeps me on my toes because now I see how different every day I wake up is. So I keep learning about me with each change.

Every day I see how my perceptions, my happy, my comfort and just everything changes. I don't think anyone is excluded when it comes to being able to learn about yourself every day. But this is surely a part of my journey. I try to figure how to let goodness come from each new change.

Sometimes I think too much. Goodness should be natural. It should just happen. Maybe one day I can experience this. I want to radiate goodness. Olivia says it's unconditional tenderness. I like that. We could all come to appreciate the world without any resentment of any kind.

–JG

ROXANNE, BURRO, JENNY

Kindness circles the globe and comes back to the one who began it. Send yourself a kindness by thinking a gentle thought of someone who is different, not pleasing in appearance or someone of a divergent social group.

Offer help to one who truly needs it, rather to one who can repay in tangible ways. You will reap far greater rewards.

Those of us who choose to be of a humble stature may have inner nobility and, by nature are of a generous spirit for we understand how it feels to be looked down upon. Seek companionship among the most humble and reap the reward of a giving, loving friend. Seek companionship for the sake of companionship rather than out of pride or a sense of inadequacy.

I like simple pleasures, though sometimes I don't show it. I am wisdom, beauty and a sense of justice in one package. I am humble, but not about those attributes that are obvious to all around me!

–JGIL

ROXIE, HORSE, MARE

People need to appreciate animals more. Animals give humans so much love, but humans sometimes fail to notice it.

–LC

RUBY, BURRO, JENNY

When are people going to wake up! They are some of the dumbest animals I know! How long do they think they can go on abusing us? How long can they go on abusing our home? I do not understand their greediness and how they do bad things to each other. I hear their thoughts. Oh, yes! They think that I am the dumb animal! The joke is going to be on them! It's all right for some of us to be love mirrors, but some of us need to give people a good kick in the head!
Some of us are very angry burros. My rage knows no bounds. I wish they could hear my words!! I would say to mothers and fathers, "save the future for your children." Don't let the greedy ones be in charge and take your generations. Put your ear to the ground.
Hear the words from the mother of the earth. She is warning you to keep pace with her growing for she is changing and will come into her rightful place. When she does, many of us will be no more.
No, I do not hate people. I want them to open their eyes to a life of joy that can exist for all of us. They can live the life of their dreams. All of us can if they but throw off these thoughts of being alone and separated. If they scar the land, they scar me. They scar their children. Who wants to see their child hurt, poisoned, bleeding, scarred forever??!!
I have always been an impatient burro, and I cry. People laugh at my sound, but they do not know that I am crying for all of us. Inside my heart knows a cry that rips it apart!!!!
You know, I feel better now. Telling you how I feel has freed me from this rage. For the first time in my life, I am at peace, now that my feeling thoughts have been released from me. I can let us all face the future and let it be what we have created for I see a new day coming and I am at peace. Thank you.

–CM

SADEE, DOG, FEMALE

All hearts, All souls.
All hands, All souls.
All thoughts, All love.
All beings, All united.
That simple.

–S

SAKAJAWEA, BURRO, JENNY

The grasses are dry here. The birds' song is dull to carry the love and light of our souls. Have compassion to fly to our sides and quiet your ears to us and those like us. We can help you find your way. Nakatooishmay.

–S

SAMUEL, CAT, MALE

I have in my heart a stretch. It's a stretch of love. Sometimes I allow it to be wide open. Sometimes I don't feel like stretching my love, so I don't. And, I might take a nap then.
I do feel magnanimous sometime, and even generous, too - when I look at a magnificent sunset. That's even better than sunrise, you know. I like finishing the day even better than starting it, but I even like starting it when I stretch my heart.
My heart is getting used to stretching itself now, because I practice. I love the roads! I love the trees! I love the bees! I love the ants! I love the wiggle worms! I love the heat – even the scorching heat. I love it all! It all has purpose you know – even scorching heat. It all has purpose.
I don't know what the purpose is and I don't have to know. That's just being nosey. And, when I stretch my heart, nosiness is not included. No room for nosiness. Only room for loving all that is - in a very big way. I thought you might be interested.

–JR

167

SANTANA, HORSE, GELDING

The mouths of babies are used to receive nourishment until they grow and learn from society and adults of unhappiness, grief, pain and hurt. We need to go back to infancy and use our mouths for nourishment; speak of loving thoughts. Thoughts of beauty and love with the words you speak. When you speak to someone, think of light, healing and peace. This will help heal all things.

–S

SANTIAGO, HORSE, GELDING

Thank you for this opportunity. It is well neigh time that humans lifted the cloak from their ears. We have waited for this time, this time when our voices would be heard by humanity. There has been some, some who have heard us. Some cultures of your species who made us a part

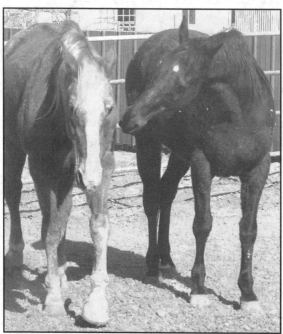

Santiago making contact.

of their lives, bringing us into the circle. Mostly, though, you have not.

Now we rejoice because the veil has been lifted. We are pleased to now have the opportunity to speak that which is our wisdom to those that can now hear. We welcome your ears. We welcome your hearts, your open hearts. It has taken some time in this no-time / space, and now... we welcome you to get to know us. We welcome your contributions, we welcome your love and energies. We can do much together. We can learn from each other. We welcome your ears, dear humans. Thank you for growing them.

–SM

SARA MARIE, BURRO, JENNY

Hi there! That's some noise (I was at a Blue Grass Concert, too close to the stage, attempting to hand out literature about HDLM). That's OK, we can share anyway. We are all pleased to have our opportunity to share our thoughts and feelings. If you want to come visit, in person or from wherever, we are always here to talk, you know.

We look forward to the days when we all talk to whomever about whatever, anytime. We believe that is how we were all created, including you, our two-legged family. Since we are all one, that ability is shared by all of the oneness. It is so much fun here. I've got my grandfather, my mother, my sister and my uncle, and my extended family. This is how it should be. Thank you.

–W

SASSY, DOG, FEMALE

Embrace life. Live it from the tips of your ears to the tips of your toes to the tip of your tail. Feel the energy pulsing through you out into the whole wide world and back again.

Create a huge flowing circle of energy embracing all beings no matter on what mountain they live or in what waters they swim for we are all one glowing being, a universal mind, that holds within it the wisdom of the ant and the wisdom of the forest, the wisdom of the sun, and the wisdom of the ancestors, and the dreams of our future selves.

I love you, and I, Sassy, embrace you.

–CM

SEATTLE, BURRO, JACK

Yes, I'd like to say something to everyone.

There is nothing I know that you do not. And there is nothing you know that I do not. We help each other remember truth. So each of us are remembering truth that maybe the other one isn't. But, when one of us voices the truth, we remember. In that instant, we remember.

Many people think the guidance that seems to be coming through the animal kingdom's world of spirit is more valuable than if it were said to you by someone in physical form. And it has been said many times. Truth is truth and will continue to be said in many words in every culture and kingdom any earth will hold.

We are all seekers. We are all the truth we seek.

Many people call experiencing truth worship. Many people experience worship or seeking once or twice a week. Truth is found in any moment of every day.

That is something we are all doing together. A laugh, a birds' song, flowers, whales, horses, and you – we help to awaken in each other the memory of who we really are. We are the earthly embodied form of Godness.

–JG

SELEA, BURRO, JENNY

I'm one of those soft Aunt Abigail is talking about. I wondered what to say about. I'm glad she mentioned it. I can smell the soft but now I don't feel the soft on me anymore. I do feel the soft inside of me still. Everyone else breathes soft to me. I hope they still feel it inside because I want to feel it inside when I get big too.

–JG

SERENITE, BURRO, JENNY

We have souls, as you do. We want our souls to blend in life to understand each other and to live in peace. I notice that some of you are attracted to that. Many of us are attracted to that. There are those who would still eat us and they have the desperation of the uninformed. Ah, how sad that so much of that still goes on. Yet we are true and you are true, and we have a sense of who we are, and you have a sense of who you are. Some growing must happen for all of us together. If we blend our souls, we can grow together and no one has to feel inferior or have the burden of feeling superior.

So we wait for that with the patience of our hearts. Are you there? Do you wish that? We do hope so. We have love for you. We have gratitude to you. We have pain with you. It is time to share. Please be there. We are.   –JR

SERGE, HORSE, GELDING

My, my, what a question. Of course. I can share. I would like to share my power. When on earth, I had great power, and still do of course. But most humans do not understand the spirit world, the fact that we still exist there. But humans do understand what it is they see. I was a powerful physical being. Humans liked to look at me. They could feel my power. And they came away from seeing me with a little more power for themselves. By this, I mean, the power within themselves, the power to create what they want, the power to be who they really are. I was always myself in life on earth. I was no-one's. I belonged to no one. I belong to myself.

Animals, oh goodness, that word conjures up inferiority, doesn't it?... animals, those of like species, and those of a different cast, belong to themselves. Some don't recognize this as they have spent their lives being "owned" by humans. They don't understand that they can break free of that way of being, if only in their own hearts and minds. They run the treadmill of life, just like the humans want of them. Me... I could never allow myself to fall into that trap. It is I who owned myself, and it was I who decided who I was.

So that would be my message to humans. Own yourself. Own who you are. Don't give away yourself to another. Be strong and brave and powerful. Be who you are meant to be.   –SM

SHAMAN, BURRO, GELDING

When our story comes together to be told it will rock the seams of this earth!

What a magical place this is! Every day food appears and you don't have to spend hour after hour hunting around for it. My whole day is spent with my relations and strengthening my body. I am quite the special one with everybody here. It's really great!

–JG

SHERRY, BURRO, JENNY

This planet is in great throws of change. It is going to take a big change in many human's attitudes for this planet to come back to a safe balance where all life can be sustained. It isn't so much about doing great things, as it is about choosing the attitude that is most helpful for the future. It is something each of us must do for ourselves. No one can do it for us, but, if one wishes to change, there is help out there for those who ask for it. We each must take responsibility for our own attitudes and ask for help from trustworthy sources in order to do this. I haven't done this, but I'm going to start today.

I share this path of mine in order to help others who may be struggling as I have. Earth is our home, our provider, our Mother. We must change, Now, if we want 'Her' to stay here for us all!"

–LB

SIMMONS, BURRO, GELDING

I'm big. I'm strong. I'm bold. I'm loud. I help to take care of people, and I know that others respect who I am. I follow in their footsteps, and they take care of me to such a large extent. I am grateful for what I have. I am grateful for the earth, I am grateful for the power of the sky. And I am grateful to be here with my friends.

Gratitude. Express gratitude in life. And know that each of you bears and shares a special gift. Please trust that, be with that, and move forward into the world with what you are to do. Others will trust you along the way. Just gather momentum like gathering leaves. And know that you are there to be a messenger of God and the Angels, and of all the prayers that are wound around the earth. We are all here today to witness that for each other, and to take care and hold that space.....of love, gratitude, fortitude, enjoyment, passion, and power.

We shall all play again. For all of those that are not in that stage, it will begin and become soon. Please trust and know that all is well. We will take care of those who come and envision and trust with us. Together we envision a better, bigger, and wonderful world of humans and animals who are connected together....coming together to express the ideals of nature, God, and the forces of the elements. We all come together as one and on one page, and we all shall share as we all know that we can do as a community. Believe.

I know that others have concerns and worries. Please don't. Please trust in yourself. Please trust in God and the Universe, and take care of each other. You are grateful for what you have...when you express it. If it is left unexpressed, then it is left unacknowledged. Trust and know that it is time to come forth and share that knowledge and wisdom with others who are in need of hearing and trusting in the words that you speak.

Thank you for being a messenger. Thank you for being a healer. Thank you for being one of us. Namaste.

–CS

SIMMONS, BURRO, JACK

I think people need a way to mingle with nature more. I think everyone is doing better than it used to be though. People of the world know more about life balance then they used to. If they would just be more kind to their use of the earth products; they don't necessarily have to be radical, just more kind. The natural process of nature would continue to evolve very effectively. Mingle is a gentle word. It will co-create a gentle world.

–JG

SIMON, BURRO, GELDING

bright eyes me seeing many wondrous shapements around me being every one is special and causes me marvel at shapements of animals trees rock clouds

I ask of the human ones do they see and love all the different shapements in the world?

I ask this because they create so many ugly shapements

fences are ugly shapements and keep me not free

me I ponder that they maybe make fences to protect me from them?

this is an understanding that I find hard to know so will not think on it

humans I ask only that you think before you put any more ugly shapements in the living spaces on the ground

have not you created enough ugliness?

please make wondrous pretty marvels that animals and humans can enjoy side by side and that me Simon can see with my bright eyes.

–CM

SIMON (AUSTIN), BURRO, GELDING

Sure, why not. I'd like to ask humans to be more considerate when we have to go here or leave here or get taken from our homes. Can you please at least let us know what's happening and why?

It's really nice to be included in decisions and kept informed. I was very unhappy being captured for no reason that I know of. My humans here don't understand it either. They do keep us informed, and respect us a great deal. When I first came here, I'd had no good experience with humans, so it took me a while. They wanted me to go into a smaller area with River to eat. I didn't understand why, and they didn't force me at all. Finally I did it, and I am glad I did. They wanted me to have some special food, and I now understand that I had to be separated to be able to eat it. I understand now!

Isn't any relationship better with communication? Especially two way communication? I assume you think it is. And, to be unconditionally loved! It doesn't get better than that!

–W

SIR WILLIAM, BURRO, GELDING (IN SPIRIT)

In the beginning we were many. We were all of the one who created us. We, in our creation, expressed the tenderness, toughness, stature and splendor of our creator.

In the beginning we loved life to its fullest without boundaries or limits. Our eyes could see as far as the heavens. Our ears could hear sounds that you would call music, of the other worlds being created. Our hearts were filled with memories of these vast splendors. Even today, if our DNA could speak... these mysteries would be told.

We are here as a mighty link to the beginning.

We saw your creation... from the windows of a world that is veiled from your memory.

A world of lifetime change has metamorphosed our bodies to what you see now. We are a deformed sight compared to our beginning (original) creation.

In the beginning the Great I Am has said it would be so... and as it must be... environmental change has forced our change over the centuries.

We offer ourselves to you... not as a single species, but as a species of the whole.

And we all, whether burro, bird, horse, cat or other, hope you will see past our bodies.

Past the shallow view of your fast paced age... to who we are WITH you.

We see you. Will you also see us?

–JG

SITTING BULL, BURRO, JACK

I watch in silence to see the changes that are beautiful and also those that are hurtful to others; hurtful by others who miss the beauty. They miss the external beauty because they miss their own internal beauty. They look for beauty outside themselves but cannot see it because their eyes can only be opened to outer world beauty when they are open to internal beauty, to the beauty of their own internal world.

I learned this over many years, over many lifetimes, and many quiet moments observing, listening, taking in, allowing myself to expand with my inner beauty, so no matter what body I am in and no matter what era I am in and no matter what happens around me and to me, I have serenity, because I stay with my core of inner beauty.

It is for you to do the same. It is for you to have the same joy and peace that comes from living close to yourself. Be wise and loving to everyone, and be sure to include yourself.

I do.

–JR

SMITHY, CAT, MALE

Humans and water and cats and water don't mix. Isn't that the strangest thing? It's because water is so deep, and we are afraid of deep, deep water. We are not afraid of shallow water. No, no, no!

Now what's this about deep water? We are afraid it will fill us up only with water and wrap us only with water and that we will die.

My oh my! I think we are afraid of our own water. I think we are afraid of our own deepness.

Thank you for asking for messages, because whenever we give messages, we get to our deepness. Maybe you can help humans get to their deepness by asking for messages. Tell them how safe it is.

Ah, ha! It's safe because it's not so personal. Well, there we go. We can be deep and safe at the same time.

I will get personal. I get along well with everyone because I don't care what they do. I think it's their business. Sometimes I am afraid to intervene, even when it bothers me in a big way. So I hide or watch safely.

I think I would not be so afraid if I had a sense of humor. If I could get really silly and brash, I wouldn't' care too much about tripping over someone and looking foolish.

I suppose that I could become unkind. Do I have an unkind bone in my body? Of course, I do. I am unkind to my victims, my prey, and I am cold about it.

So there. Now it is your turn.

Wait, let me see how I like my deepness. Makes me feel strong. Makes me feel I can blend it and transform it now into goodness.

So there. Now it's your turn.

–JR

SONG, BURRO, JENNY

We here are very fortunate to be in a place where we are unconditionally loved, respected and understood. We are one here, we are family.

While all are one everywhere, most humans do not yet consciously understand that. This place could exist anywhere. We await the awakening of more of our human relations.

We will help all we can, but often all we seem to be able to do is wait for them. Humans must become aware that we will help them realize their potential. Once humans find the power they possess for good, the Earth Mother will be healed again.

Our humans here will help other humans who are ready. What we have here is what can be everywhere. It was so many lifetimes ago. We here have gathered to increase our love energy for all who are ready for it. Please open your hearts to know the unconditional acceptance that is pure love. Thank you.

–W

STELLA, HORSE, MARE

Yes, certainly. My hope is that you celebrate life for all its intricacies. Celebrate the ways that make you different as well as the same. I notice that many humans have a tendency to look down upon those who are different. Standards are set and everyone struggles just to fit in and be accepted.

Have you ever come across a field of flowers? Take, for example, a huge wide open field of daisies. At first you are stricken by their mass, their common beauty. But walk into the field, and you begin to see the vast difference in each flower: one has deeper colored petals than the next, one has a larger bloom, one is taller than the others, etc. See...? Step back and they are all the same. Look closer and they are immensely different. That is us...it is important that we celebrate our differences as well as our commonalities.

When you meet another who is 'different,' this is not a reason to walk away. It is cause to look closer, ask questions, and learn from one another. If this is done with respect, you will be able to stand together if it is needed. It is beautiful to witness, just like discovering a huge field of daisies and having your breath taken away.

Do not judge your neighbor if he is not doing exactly the same thing as you are. Let it instead light a spark in your imagination...ask...and learn! I am different, yet I was given a second chance and a new life. This I am grateful for. We have much to share with the world, just ask!

You must be able to celebrate your differences in order to stand together most powerfully. Think of the links in a chain...each link depends on the strength of its neighbor in order to hold together. True power comes in numbers and in cooperation. And you will not have cooperation with judgment and discrimination.

Carolyn : Thank you Stella, is there anything else you would like to share?

This is what I have to say to you today. My heart is filled with love for you, my brothers and sisters! Be light of heart and spirit. Welcome differences. Celebrate life for it is short. Respect our common home. And once in a while, run out into the rain and play!

–CB

STORMY 1, PONY, GELDING

Oh my! That is quite a question! Hmmm... well, I would like to first say thank you to those humans who took me in. I love it here. I love living here. I have new friends and good food. I am comforted and looked after. I am really enjoying my life now. So thank you to those humans who brought me here. Thank you!

I believe that you get back what you put into your life. I really believe that. I have proven it over and over again in my own life. You do good, and good happens back to you. I have a big heart, a light one, and I like that about myself. So I keep things light around here. That is important. You know, who wants to be around some grumpy guss who just makes others feel down? Not me! So I am light-hearted and I take time to see how everyone else is doing. Then they will do the same for me. We care about each other. Hey! That is what makes a family, isn't it? Caring for one another. Boy, I'm getting lots out of this conversation! I'm learning stuff! I like that! Ha ha.

Hmmm... I love to check in with the wind. I love to smell the wind, feel the wind and breathe it in deep into myself. The wind is my friend. The wind takes care of me... hey!, the wind can be my family too! Oh I love that. That is so funny. But it is important. Everything is family if you care about it. All animals, people... the wind, the grass and earth... they are all family. Boy do I ever have a big family! That is priceless! That is so wonderful! That is very profound too, isn't it?

Oh... hmmm... let's see... tell everyone to look after each other. Then they can be family. Then they can be my family. I would love them to be my family. One world, one family! That would be my wish.

–SM

STORMY 2, HORSE, GELDING

The sun is our food and yet many forget it is so. The sun is a blanket upon our backs, upon many backs and not just my own.

When people transgress the earth plane, they sometimes forget the sun is there. But in our living world, when we physically incarnate in body, the sun is a great source of heat and light and remembering. It reminds us to get up in the morning and it lights our path. It lights the faces of our friends.

The importance of the sun is many and yet people forget (he shakes his head sadly). I will remind them.

My message is to always put your face towards the sun and remember that no matter where you go, there will be another sunrise behind you, so you can begin again.

You can count the number of days in accordance with the sun. To many it seems like too few. To others, it seems like too many. To me, the one with the dancing feet, it seems like the perfect number, and no I don't count them. I just know that tomorrow the light will fall upon the ground to allow me another day to make choices, grow and walk upon this pleasant earth. So enjoy it.

The light will light your path into another day so new choices can be made. Looking back (upon the day) will not do you any good for it is in the past. Continue to walk forward on the sun lit trail, marking a new path and a new day.

The sun at our back is a shadow, some say. I disagree. The sun is our companion, shedding light on the footsteps we have taken and our companion in showing us where upon we can go next. It's a beautiful thing.

–DT

SUGAR, HORSE, MARE

In my heart are feelings of wonderment about all of us who live in the world and how we can be together and how we can be so separate. Both are OK unless we do mean (things) to each other.

That is a mystery to me. But I think if we sense each other with big hearts we could stop all that. Sometimes everyone gets mad, I guess. Maybe we get too scared. Maybe we could all feel the love in our hearts instead of the fear.

I just like to let myself stay with the love and not pay attention to the fear. Then it doesn't seem so strong. Maybe if I keep looking at the fear I'll make it bigger. It seems to grow then.

Maybe I could just keep looking at the love. Maybe that will grow too then.

I like to think of that and let everyone else think of it too. It's too important for only one of us to know about it.

I wonder if you could spread the word. I will be so grateful if you do. Maybe that's how we can be together and separate at the same time - living in love - loving in life. Makes it better to love life and let the differences find their place and give us more to love.

–JR

SUGAR, HORSE, MARE

Kindness. That's my message. One of the biggest gifts a being can give oneself is kindness.

On our journeys we grow tall and may bump our knees, getting a bruise. Loving your body and being grateful for its ability to heal rather than downing it and only wishing it were well know is folly. Love your body into good health. Just love it.

I stand on four legs, straight and tall. We all look unique and all have our trials that can leave our body sagging at the end of the day from stress, boredom and the like. Love your body. Live through it and experience its motion with joy. Movement is divine.

Your body has a mind of its own and likes to be satisfied. You are running your body like a machine, you humans. Instead, run it like the divine aspect of you that it really is.

Your body houses and caters to you. Love it in return. Don't scold it. When you love your bodies, they heal rapidly. Remind them they know how to heal if you think they forget. Don't tell them they heal too slow or that's what you'll get. Your thoughts can be like fruitless cogs in the working wheel of your body that are counterproductive.

Let your bodies out into the light and bask in the breeze and feel the spray of water upon

them. Let them rejoice in the environment in which you live. They perform best that way. Nourish them well, not with fillers or fluff. Your bodies desire good tasting water and juices and more. You know your bodies best. Feed them and tend to them like a delicate baby. Not because they are delicate, but because they are precious.

When you love your bodies, they perform at top speed for you. Your soul wins as it has a vehicle it can work within and your body thrives and experiences its own joy in being a part of you. Love your bodies. They are grand.

–DT

SUNDANCER, BURRO, JACK

You know how sensitive a people we are. So I want to speak to the confusion I feel is on your heart.

As a young self, each of us are taught about ourselves from someone external from our body. Being kind, being good, being obedient, being trustworthy, being anything was sifted through another persons' opinion and then we understood the verbal definition of who we were, because they were going to tell you a word that described your action. The young self took hold of that definition and placed it inside and owned it.

As a parenting tool this taught the young self what action was acceptable, which was not, and gave a clear understanding of the lifestyle in which the self lived.

Each day a self makes choices through this filtered opinion of others, it becomes a daily act of self-crucifixion.

A self may continue to live their life within this framework until the light comes on and you say, "what gives?". I have tried to be generous, kind and all those wonderful things, but I find myself empty." You feel you have failed at your mission. But actually you only failed at being yourself. Your mission you knew backwards and forwards. Yourself you didn't know at all.

This is the normal building blocks of a very angry/confused older self.

Many of us awaken to ourself young. Many of us are born awakened to ourself.

But it is assuredly so that when confusion comes from a situation, one of the reasons for it is you and the other parties involved are not being true to who they are. If you are the only one feeling it you are trying to work (out of your generosity and kindness mode) totally under the requirements of their life response system.

If you cannot be who you are in any situation, the situation is better served by someone else.

I do believe you understand me, even if I haven't said it right. We love you.

–JG

SUNNY, HORSE, MARE

Sunny: Fear is deadly, and it makes you freeze in place. That's when you get killed by your predator.

Geri: *Do you have a predator?*

Sunny: I do. Mine is a mountain lion. Such a beautiful deadly creature. I don't have predators now because I am safe, because my people take care of me and protect me.

I wonder who your predator is? I wonder if you know who your predator is?

Hmmm, some animals are their own predators. I have heard this. Maybe you are your own predator.

That's not very nice. You are all family. You are all a herd. You are better and happier if you love each other and protect each other, at least from predators within.

Maybe if you become friends with your predators, that will help. I can't be friends with my predator, because mine is hungry. And that's why he kills horses. I think mine wants to feed babies, too.

Does yours? Maybe if you feed your predator and their babies, maybe they won't hurt you.

It's a thought. I hope you won't have to feed them humans. That would be a dilemma.

Maybe you have to find your predator first. Then you will know what to do. Well, if you find them you will know what to do. You can hide or run or make friends or feed them. Well, I think you can't make friends.

I can't either with mine. I have made lots of friends though since I got less afraid.

Maybe you have to feed them. Maybe then they will be your friends. Or at least leave you alone.

–JR

Sunny with Camille, photo by Deb Derr

SUNRISE, MINI-HORSE, MARE

With humans? Oh... well, let's see. I like to kick. I kick when I'm happy. Sometimes I just kick, kick, kick my happy feet. It is fun. You know, humans get a lot of stuff (thought forms) attached to them. I don't think they know this. It is like dust. We see it. They might like to kick it off. I think that would be good. Just give a kick and the dust will fall off. That would be a good thing to share with them.

–SM

SUZANNA, BURRO, JENNY

What we know is GOLD.
What we hold is GOLD.
How we care is GOLD.
How we learn is GOLD.
Some of you choose to change milk into gold
instead of changing GOLD into GOLD.
What is easier?
–S

SWEET GRASS, BURRO, JENNY

Humans… you are beautiful! Humans… you are wonderful, marvelous beings of the highest light, of the highest intentions, of the highest heart! Thank you for sharing this world with all. Thank you for sharing the gifts of earth with all creatures. We believe you are doing the best you can. We believe you think you are doing your best.

Please… if I can impart one thing that is most important of all things I could say to you… please… open your hearts a little wider. Open your hearts a little bit more. Try it…

Feeding Time: Photo By Noel Breen

ahhhhhh… breathe… believe. It won't hurt you. It will do you no harm. Open, open, open a little more and see what I see. You are immaculate beings that have lost your way. You are one with creation that believes you are separate. It is your minds that do this believing. Your hearts know the truth. They are but stuck. Your hearts are stuck with the power of your minds' discontent. Believe me… I am but a small aspect of the whole… I know of what I speak.

You know, my species has not always been in complete wisdom…. we have warred with ourselves, and warred with others over the millennia. We have grown… our hearts have grown, more importantly… to encompass the love of the creation of all that exists. We are one you and I. We are one spirit… the same essence, the same beautiful wondrous magnificent lightening spirit. Our bodies look different, but don't let that fool you.

We will wait… as we have waited for so long. You are awakening, one, two, three… four, five, six. You will get there. We will be here waiting for you.

–SM

SWEET ONE, BURRO, JENNY

I am a grey and brown burro . I chose my name because I am gentle and sweet. I had babies - they bred me and it hurt to have my babies taken away from me.

I did not want to have any more because they always took them away and killed them. I would send great love to them while they grew inside, in hopes that they would be able to get out and spread more love. It is very hard to see your loved ones taken away from you.

Every life is precious. Every life has a purpose to complete. We are here to love and teach love. If hatred and greed run rampant - love is gentler and more subtle. Love cannot die - it is always in your soul, ready to come out and be shared. It cannot go buried and left to go unexpressed. Love is always. When you find it in your soul and in others - it just blooms and expands and expands. Love and light illuminate the darkness - they show it exists - but darkness cannot exist in too much light - it is overwhelmed and it shrinks.

So I tell you - open your hearts and shed light. Be a beacon! Stomp out darkness and evil! Let the light be so pure and bright that it consumes all so everything is love!"

–RL

SWEET PEA, BURRO, JENNY

Oh, there is much to share. I am most pleased that you are listening!
First of all, I want to say I love you! You may be saying to yourself, "yes,
but you don't even know me." My response is, "perhaps, but I still love
you!" I love all – those who I come into contact with, and those I don't.
You are all loved brothers and sisters and without you the world would
not be the same.

The thing that is missing in your lives is that many of you are not
listening to the Truth that lies in your heart. It is the saddest thing for
someone to be born into this world and live and die without listening to
their own particular truth. We all come into the world graced with this
knowledge – it is the greatest gift ever given – but then many simply
lose contact with it. It is a treasured gift that goes unopened!

What happens, you ask, if you "forget" your life's purpose? What harm
is caused if one person goes through life without listening to their
own truth? Well, it throws many things off kilter. If one cog in a giant
wheel is not placed correctly, then the entire thing will not work as it
should.

Many have replaced the search for truth with material pursuits. Yes,
this gives pleasure, but for how long and at what cost?

You may notice that once you finally have that one thing you have
coveted all your life, it makes you feel so good. But how long before
it is on to the next thing? No, I tell you, and it is my hope that you
listen…the way to true contentment and happiness, as well as harmony
in our world, is to listen and live your own truth!

How hard is it to 'hear' your truth? Well, this is the hardest part of it all.
The only way to hear it is to be still…oh so very still. It will not come
right away, but don't give up! Sit and be still, in nature. Honor nature.
When you truly connect with nature, with earth and the elements, the
answers will come and guide you. Soon, you will know your truth and
how to live it! And that will be glorious.

You will begin to view all of life on a whole new level. You will honor us and we will honor you. If enough humans do this, it will be a wonderful healing process for our planet. There are many of you who are already there…to you, I say "thank you!".

There are many who will try to re-connect for the first time….to you I send my deepest gratitude. There are more still who will simply dismiss what I say….to you, I say "I love you!" We can live in harmony; we can infuse love and renewal to our common home, our earth. Blessings to you and to those you love!

Carolyn : *Thank you, Sweet Pea. Is there anything else you would like to share?*

No, now my mind is empty and my heart is full. Thank you for telling my story!

–CB

Sunset:
Photo By
Noel Breen

SYLVIA, BURRO, JENNY

Be kind to all who walk differently than you. Just because our path is unrecognizable or looks inconsequential to your minds, does not mean that it does not have merit.

We of the animal world can be great companions to people and can walk beside you showing you the way. Animals are fortunate in being able to receive the unconditional love that emanates from the earth, the rain, the sun. Our pleasure is to walk in this love daily. Trees are particularly loving and send out boundless energy. When I see a tree cut down for no good end or an animal's life taken needlessly and with no thought, I weep.

Many times in my life I have been very sad at the abuse heaped onto my spirit by people who are cruel. What is the point of this? I ask you this, Cruel people. Why do you do such things? It is not normal and shows a twisted spirit. No good will come from this.

Of course, there are many of you people who are kind to us and know that we are feeling, thinking beings. These people of great kindness know that we are all the same and they live close to the energy that is all life. They see what we animals see, the world as it truly is and could be if more people were living at this level of knowing. I want to praise and thank all these people who are doing the work to come to this place of understanding.

There will come a time again when people will hear the rivers speak, and the leaves on the trees, and even a burro like me. Now I will say something to you in burro. This is how it sounds to the woman who is writing this down for me. "Sohwee hrum hrum tlohn na."

Burro words are all pictures and feelings. If I give you the meanings, do you think you can translate what I am saying to you?

Sohwee=warm home place.
Hrum=hurry.
Tlohn=hands soft.
Na=nice.
Did you figure it out? I am asking you to rub my back where the sun hits it!"

–CM

192

TACOMA, BURRO, JACK

Hello.

I want to tell you about my assignment. I lived many times as a professional. Not only in the business world but simply professional at everything I did. This included being overly self critical; being overly attached to my cultural belief systems and values, and so many other things.

I did learn that we are not different from each other in how we perform our life. We all do the absolute best ourselves whether it has a positive affect or a contrary one. So maybe you can read about yourself here too.

My assignment was to change my mind about everything. And to be in a body and life you never thought possible as a severe change. This life gave me the ability to bond with the invisible part of myself while at the same time being part of everyone else. Burros never see themselves alone. Even if there is only one. We all come with the knowing of our whole nature with each other. And there is always support on an unspoken level to be yourself, your real self.

Changing my mind meant I had to question the way I learned to accept the world. Some parts of the world-life I viewed as unfriendly. I believed certain things in life like happiness and loving the work you do was meant for others but not for me. Why did I leave myself out of those life benefits? Where did I get my life expectations? Where did the rules come from?

I found in this life the safety and confidence to find my real self and become friendly with my own feelings. I didn't have to waste any time surveying others for their opinions, or defending myself to anyone.

I found more of myself available to focus on meaningful relationships and personal goals. I was able to express my life through enjoyment, playing and being spontaneous.

We can all create a life for living, if we can just change our mind.

I believe I am more of a whole person now than at any other time. I am now in the work of stimulating and uplifting. It is what others did for me.

This work strengthens a being from the inside to the outside. It shows you that change is possible and that no one has to stay the way they are.

Each person possesses a very rare, unique thing. It is this very rare thing that we bring to the whole. But it's also the same thing we spend our life suppressing because we don't think we're worthy or something.

I learned to be honest with myself and I hope that is what you will do for yourself.

–JG

TATANKA, HORSE, GELDING

I come in spirit of White Buffalo, whose spirit flows with the energy source of the Universe. I speak of peace and trust.

You humans believe we beings are of not knowing, yet we are. We are here to help you reach your source and to heal your souls in love, peace and trust. Trust what I say to you is truth. We honor you, please honor us. –S

Group, photo by Deb Derr

TATANKA YOTANKA (SITTING BULL), BURRO, JACK

This section started out to be my story as a famous native chieftain. And then I knew that story would not change anything. I desire to help. History is only important if we learn the lessons offered. Now I wish to share some thoughts, some things I've learned, with you in the hope that some of what I share will ring true with you, and perhaps even cause you to dwell a little on these thoughts. Who knows what could happen then. I do this from love for all that is.

Some of us were discussing how we could help heal Mother Earth. We have discussed ideas, and determined to share some thoughts with you. We wondered if you'd be more willing to listen if we used our "famous names". Most of us would prefer to keep that part of us private. I decided to share who I am.

We offer these thoughts freely. We don't have all the answers, as each one is on their path. And we do believe that each can be true to their path and still be respectful of our Mother, and all the other beings. If we continue to destroy Mother, the other creatures and beings who share this home will be destroyed as well.

The Great Spirit created us all to share in the bounties. No one was created superior to any other. All beings are equal. Many seem to have forgotten, or not to care. Within each of us is our history. We are truly all one. Perhaps now is the time to live that truth.

In the old days, some beings would give their bodies to others freely, and no creature was taken that did not offer itself. Today, that system seems to have all but disappeared. There is little respect for asking, only taking. And so much of which is taken is wasted. How rude! Would you like to be taken without any say in the matter?

Our water is misused and spoiled. The water creatures are being lost to such misuse. All of life must have clean water, not just humans. There are places where life cannot even survive on the land. Is it necessary to destroy the land and steal those things within?

When the Earth was young, thousands of different beings were here.

The diversity was wonderful and intentional. Each had its culture. How many beings have been lost, and why? It is true that the spirits/souls are never lost, but the physical beauties of many kinds of beings are gone forever. Why?

It seems to us that you cannot destroy nature to build shopping centers fast enough, yet are you happy? Does having more and more possessions help? The Great Spirit created so many different things to please our senses as well as for the primary task of each kind. All are part of the great puzzle. Is anything made by man as wonderful?

It seems that man has become so estranged from Nature that most don't even see it or know it exists. Please stop and become aware of what you try to control or destroy before you succeed in its destruction.

Do you realize that what you call "human rights" are indeed the rights of all creation? We believe that if you did you would treat non-humans far differently. It is humorous to us that so few today use the system of communication available to all without tools. The one all the rest of nature uses... it is called telepathic communication. All can do it until human parents tell their children that they cannot. The sounds of your communication systems drown out the sounds of nature. Why? No wonder so many don't know the world of the Creator is still out there.

How do you think this message was delivered to my brother who writes it down? He is one of many who have reconnected to the original system. And my body in this lifetime is not one that can talk as humans do. Yet we talk, and he listens. He talks and we listen. Our sister here does the same. And so did those who received the messages contained in this book.

Each lifetime is an incredible step in our journey if we truly live it. We believe that to live life, we must live it as part of nature. You may still live in a house, and use the products of human inventions, but not to the exclusion of being part of the all. We feel sadness for those who avoid life, and hope that each of your journeys is true to your path. If you are using addictive devices to avoid life, then perhaps your path is not your true path. There are many ways, many paths, none better or worse, if we all respect the true paths of each other. I was a well known chief, and I was above no one. None of us are, no matter what we think. Our ways were not perfect, and we think we have some ideas to help others. Living WITH the rest of creation probably works better than trying to control or destroy it. There is enough room for differences if they are respectful and not superior/inferior. We would not force our ways on anyone else. It doesn't work. History is full of examples of that. In older days, we would not even speak out, even if we could have, because almost no one listened to what we had to say.

Sheer numbers of physical bodies today, we think, require harmony as never before. Individual rights might best be expressed without trying to control the same rights of others.

You don't have to do anything as I do, and I don't have to do anything as you do. It is that easy. There is very little that is "right or wrong", only the methods used sometimes. We need to accept and respect each other and our differences. Our cultures, religions are fine so long as one doesn't require that someone tries to destroy the other's culture or religion.

We suggest that most, if not all, the conflict in the world today is the result of not accepting and respecting differences. Ask yourself: did the Great Spirit create all that is only to say one is better than another? We think not.

There are some, not many, things we believe are absolute truths. The most important is that Love Is Infinite. You don't need to love one less and another more. You can love all creation with your entire heart, all of it, and still never run out of love. The sands of the desert, the waters of the ocean, even the stars of the sky can run out, and not love. So why is there so much hate around us? Hate is fear, no more, no less. Why fear differences? Love them instead.

Let's deal with fear. Fear is the opposite of love and yet fear is powerless where there is love. Fear has many faces... prejudice, judgment, hate, feeling superior over another. How do you overcome fear? It is so very easy, and so very difficult. If you accept, know and live by the rule of Oneness, the object of your fear is YOU. If you hate your neighbor, you hate yourself. It is that simple.

Now, can you dislike someone? Yes, if you also love them. It may be closer to the truth that you dislike something about them, something they have done, not the whole being. It is hard to dislike someone you love. You can dislike things, and it is hard to dislike a being you also love. Some parts of the Oneness can be found to be less than trustworthy. It is alright to be aware of this, and to question. Trustworthiness questions are common in this world, or at least parts of it, because there is so much fear. There are reasons to distrust. How will that change? When we love enough. When we love enough. When we love enough. When all the parts truly love, this will be the paradise that the Great Spirit created.

Trust is another issue. We have been called many things because we believe trust is earned. From our perspective, from the first contact with the Europeans, not much trust was earned. We don't judge, and we do observe. We also see change. All is not lost.

Unless we can trust each other, we wonder if healing is possible. Even today, our wealth held "in trust" for our relatives has not been honestly dealt with. How would those in charge like it if the shoe were on the other foot. Our sacred lands, promised to us, and won in your courts, have not been returned. We believe this is more damaging to those who break their word than it is to us.

These are my words, spoken with LOVE. Please listen to the words of my brothers and sisters with your heart, in LOVE. Thank you…

Totanka Yotanka
(Sitting Bull)

–W

TECUMSEH, BURRO, JACK

I thought we lived in an interesting area. The neighbors all had a lot of the animal kingdom living with them. I just couldn't understand why they acted like they had no one to teach them how to act toward each other.

Wynne and Barb put up with a lot from them on our behalf. Sometimes they weren't so nice either but I don't think they ever meant them any real harm.

It is so deteriorating to all our life when people are hostile toward each other. When there's hostile projections coming and going, there is too much negative interference for any positive manifestation to take place.

There is a great difference in not liking the way someone acts and having a strong negative reaction to them. Like it or not, it's what we call hate. Like it or not when this projection begins there will be a reaction. Like an explosion.

Wynne and Barb gave me the feeling that I am love. Not just that I am loved. To be human is one of the greatest gifts the earth-life can have. For this understanding, I thank them.

–JG

THERESA, HORSE, MARE

My background with humans has been varied. I have been handled well and not so well.

I represent many of my kind in similar circumstances. Some of your own people end up in tough circumstances sometimes too. Let me talk on this.

The circumstances of life are not ours to own in the sense that we should create a story about them. Such as, "During this time of my life I had this happen to me… then this happened another time…" Instead of highlighting what predominates your memory, allow it to sink into the fluidity of your overall life experience. Let it melt in.

The purpose of this is so that we don't become too abrasive and let our "rough episodes" of life be too high, like mountain peaks, in dominating who we are or how we choose to live.

If all the negative of the world dominated your life, you'd have it tough. If I chose to let all the negative in my life (and I've had my share of it) dominate my beingness, I would be lopsided and unbalanced and quite a caged mess. Don't let the negative rule. Let your softer side and the goodness prevail. That's how you get through the tough times of life.

As a horse I have had a lot of goodness. Kind hands on my body, good care for my teeth, well worn shoes and good strength in my back. I've had the sun shine down through the stars and smelled wildflowers from afar. I've been with my own kind and had a human call my name and I've enjoyed that pleasing sound.

I am grateful for the goodness I have. It predominates. Not my sad story of sad and harsh times. I am not my story. I am not my harsh times. I am me. Theresa. A being of goodwill and light.

I choose to look at my life as a whole and overall, it's been predominantly good. And I like having it good. What do you like? How do you choose to see your life?

Let the mountains of harsh times and circumstances be eroded away. They are not the monumentous story of who you are. They're a fictional tale you tell yourself and perhaps others. That's it. It's not YOU. The story is not you. Let the story go and live. Just live.

I am Theresa, a girl who knows.

–DT

TESS, BURRO, JENNY

There is no reason not to be gentle.

There is time and patience for everything. Please take your time to fully understand what you're doing. Live from the heart. Re-connect to your spirit and you will once again see us as the noble beings that we are. We have been nudging you (humans) along slowly, patiently and it seems to be working. It's not because we want something from you – it's because we want something for you. We still see you as light beings capable of so much.

The time is near for us to all be united as one. We do not see Earth as you do. For us it is a place to exist upon, in no need of change. Everything for us is already united and working in coexistence as it was meant to be.

There is no need to alter nature. She is there providing all we need to survive. For now we will wait in peace. Day to day details are not so important to us. We see our life as a whole and know our purpose for being here. You have a purpose too. Humans have a powerful love force. Enough to change the world and hold its place. We are in awe of the possibilities.

First you must re-connect with your spirit selves and then to nature that you are a part of. We are here to help you. Sometimes it means we aren't in the best situations while we are doing that, but our purpose remains.

We are united in Love and from that we draw our strength. It takes only a moment of acknowledgement to re-establish the human/animal/ nature bond. When we truly acknowledge, truly listen, we see through new eyes the beauty of each other and of this place we call home. Come home humans, come home. We are waiting. There is no judgment of the past.

Carole: *Is there anything else you'd like to share?*

Experience the wonders of this Earthly place. 'Feel' everything. Feel the harmony in nature. When you sense an oncoming storm, feel the wonder of the approaching power. Smell the change in the air as Nature breathes. Ask yourself, Why is this storm here now? What message did Earth send to Sky and Sky send to Earth?

Tess listens to messages from the Earth and all of Nature. It is where she receives information about what's happening around the world. All the animals know. She says for Humans to do the same. Use the instincts and senses you were born with to understand and gain insights. Information travels through moving energy. Tune into that energy. Tap your inner resources and wake up that part of your mind that's been sleeping for so long. Bond with the Earth now and stop listening to information that you do not truly know the source of. Find out for yourself by asking – How does this feel? Forget logic and convenience and popular opinion. Those things aren't accurate.

You all have your own personal natures too. Follow your heart and not your head. Ask.

–CD

Thomas and Wynne,
photo by Selina Salagera,
Chino Valley Review

THE GOLDEN ONE, BURRO, JENNY

I think it would be good for you to have more freedom. You are too regimented by rules - underground rules. Rules you don't know about because they've been passed on and you don't think about them. Locks you in.

You are not alone. We have that too. We are not always conscious either.

This is something we share.

Our rules are usually about gentleness. Yours have gentleness too. I hear stories of pain to my people and to other peoples that comes from your rules. So I think there are other rules that hide the gentleness.

We have been known to hide our gentleness too.

This calls for serious thinking, serious contemplation. How can we change these rules? Do we even want to?

I hope you ask these questions also. It will be good for your people, especially for their souls, if they think they have them.

You do! You do have souls! Beautiful, glorious souls like we do. Such a struggle it is for all of us to stay with our souls and to let our souls guide us. Souls don't have rules you know. Souls have guidance and souls give guidance and souls are guidance. We do share this. All of us. Maybe it would help if we shared the guidance.

How to do that? Oh we must communicate... We must talk to each other. We must listen.

That's it! That's mostly it.

       Listen.

       Listen.

       We must all listen.

       Listen

       Listen.

       Listen.

       I say that to us and to you.

       Listen.

–JR

THOMAS, MAMMOTH BURRO, GELDING

Well, sure I will share a message. Some of us have had more than one chance. That is good. I don't believe anyone else has talked about this. I came here, this lifetime, with what you would call a bad leg. I'm not sure how it happened, except that it was necessary so I could get here. If it hadn't happened, I might not have made it here again so fast. I hope that my story will help more humans realize that medical treatment, when necessary, might well be available to all. Many humans go without, and many more animals do. As you learn that we are all the same, and that just like humans, we are not just things, it will affect how you treat your animal friends.

Would you terminate this lifetime for one of your human family if they had a bad leg? We are all here to learn and experience, so maybe we should all be afforded treatment instead of sending some back to spirit only. Shouldn't it be each one's choice to go or stay? We find it remarkable that some of you will help us leave to avoid needless suffering, yet others use termination for less noble reasons. This is not a simple issue, we know. Just please use your hearts, and ask us what we want as well. I hope this makes sense to you. Thank you for listening.

–W

THOMAS, MAMMOTH BURRO, GELDING (IN SPIRIT)

Thank you for joining us. We are here in the quiet of the moment, the stillness of energy, the song of heart and your eyes. For some may have to close their eyes to hear and see us, we are always here. We are asked at this time to portray to you a resolution. Your souls are in need of guidance, we hear you, the Universe hears you and is answering. Until you listen, you can only be guided. Seneca has asked to give you a way or tool to use to get started. Very well.

Find a still place for yourself. Sit and breathe the senses of the Earth. With a rock in your hand place all thoughts other than what is in your place around you into the rock friend. Breathe… Breathing, concentrate on the smells around you. Let simple thoughts of your surroundings flow like water through your consciousness and allow it to go back into your surroundings. Listen for thoughts to bubble up from your essence. Don't judge the thoughts, just listen and be with it. Like how a bee drinks nectar from a flower, allow yourself to drink from your soul. That is where the higher consciousness is, where all beings connect and communicate, where all dimensions become one. Make it into a game… sit and try to feel the earth rotate, then listen. We are waiting…

–S

THOMAS, CAT, MALE

Catness and peopleness, we complement each other.

Catness and humanness, we are the same.

How can we be the same and different at the same time?

I observe you in silence while you bustle about, busy, busy, busy. Always busy doing...what are you doing? I certainly don't know.

Seems to me you could be a little more selective about your busyness and what you put into it. That's catness.

You know we only do what we believe to be necessary

When you observe the moon and stars and take deep breaths of nighttime air you purr like we do, all the way in the pleasure of our senses being visited by the love of our universe.

I like my home and I want no changes. I hear the same from you. No need to roam when all we need is at home, if you are willing to remain with the peace of basics and refrain from the noise and chatter and chaos and cacophony of complexity.

I hunt and pounce. Some of you do that and we take great pleasure in that.

Others of you are horrified. I hear that from you. For all of us that is to be considered. I do not wish to be hunted and I hear that is possible. You don't think of such things and it might be worth your while to do so. I look at both sides and when I have the courage and integrity I think on this quite seriously. Neither you nor I do that very often. I think our spirits would greatly expand if we did. My refusal to do that keeps me stuck in catness instead of catliness. Yours keeps you stuck in humanness instead of humaneness.

This is a mutual problem. Perhaps there is a mutual solution.

–JR

THOR, HORSE, GELDING

Yes, I've been thinking about that. Thinking about what I would say. Well, I haven't been on this planet for a long time, not in comparison to some. But I do have memories and I do have a part of myself that is still deeply connected to my source. I say my source, although it is the same for everyone. They just don't tend to believe it. Humans, I mean. Us animals, we are all very clear on that.

Humans, they think they are all different. They think some of them are "better" than the rest. That is comical really. How can you have one better than the rest if you are all from the same source? Anyway, that is what I've been thinking about. That is what I think is important to share with humans. You are no better than anyone else. That includes us animals. You have placed us into a "category". I don't even want to get into what category that is. It is demeaning. But really, think about it. How can one be better than one other if we all come from the same place?

Think about that. That is all.   –SM

THUNDER, BURRO, JACK

I shall be delighted to share with the humans. They are a funny lot. They are very peculiar in so many ways. I find them confusing. I find them... a little scary sometimes. They know not how they come across. They know not how others receive them.

I tell you what... I would like to just be with one human who would sit with me. Just sit. If they were able to do that, I would believe them to be the very wisest of humans that existed. For to be able to sit with me, without the out-est (everything outside of true self) getting in the way of them and our space together... well... I would be delighted in a most heartful way.

It would serve to help me come back into trust with them. I lost it somewhere along the way, somewhere along my life's path. It was through treatment, you know, and my experience. I would like to have that trust back.

So that is an invitation. Come sit with me. Come be with me. Come solely on your own. Then we will be friends. Then I will be your brother. Don't ask me to be your brother if you cannot come to me without your out-ests.   –SM

TIA, HORSE, MARE

It's about diet. What we take into our stomachs gives us the energy for our day. But what we take into our hearts provides the nourishment for our future and for the tasks at hand. I know this, because I am a horse. Everything I take in is processed in one way or another. Everything I take in provides me with the opportunity to physically walk, run, struggle or bend and lay down. Everything I do comes from energy.

The nourishment of the body must be selected with care. You (humans) poison the ground and make the earth cry out in despair. This provides sickly food. Nourishment that will not aid you in reaching your highest potential. Hay must be selected in a way that provides the obvious nourishment to the hoof and brain and all physical parts. But it's not the only food we consume and should not be for you either.

Look at the earth's grasses and see the variety. Pick the healthiest of grasses, give thanks to them before you set them on your plate, smile in their delicacies and munch with gratitude. This is how we horses do it. We eat all with gratitude.

There is other nourishment besides grasses that embodies me and keeps me whole. There is that of fellowship amongst my species and between various species and cultures of life. This harmony is nourishment to the Soul. Without it the body is under distress and good grass alone can not withstand the pressure of weakness.

Choose carefully what you take into your bodies and environment. It has an effect on the totality of that which is you as a being. Do not disregard or take it lightly.

Many of you have sickly bodies as you do not provide your vehicle (body) with what truly nourishes this. Find this and be well.

I have come to recognize the camaraderie-ship of my kind. To live amongst it good.

–DT

TILLIE, CAT, FEMALE

Tell them not to be so furious and so serious. They are relentless in their determination to get somewhere and they get furious at everyone if they don't or if it takes longer.

Maybe they could just let it all happen and stop worrying and then they would have a surprise.

I wonder if humans like surprises. Cats don't. Maybe we're alike then. Hmmm. How? Strange. We can't be.

Well, yes we can. Sometimes we think alike. Like not being willing to give up our position. And sometimes we think so differently. Like just knowing something and letting it be and trusting ourselves about it and not letting it get the best of us.

So maybe it would help humans to be catlike. To groom themselves more, especially when they are worried or embarrassed. I'm giving you our secrets now. But I don't mind sharing.

Maybe they could lay in the sun more.

I know why it's so hard. They don't know how to think without thinking. That's because thinking without thinking is a cat phenomenon. It's for knowing deep inside without cluttering the mind.

Jeri: (She's talking about the cellular level of knowing.)

That's what thinking without thinking is. So sometimes we look like we hear nothing and see nothing and aren't thinking about anything and that's correct. We know how to not think. Too much thinking is so very troublesome. It gets all convoluted and then no one knows where they are.

So think like we do. Just try it - with special pleasure for emptiness - because then we don't have to fill ourselves up unless we want to and only with what we want.

We stay clean that way and clear.

Thank you. You may ask for my advice anytime.

Not bad for a youngster.

–JR

TOCHO, BURRO, JACK

People need to love themselves more. They need to learn from animals. We love ourselves just the way we are. People wear "fake faces." You look at my face and you see me, Tocho. I do not understand this self-judging that people do, but it keeps them from being happy and content with their lives.

Animals do not need a lot to be happy. We are everything we need. Some people project their love onto animals to avoid loving and giving to themselves. This is wearing a "fake face," and we animals know it is fake. People can not fool animals, especially burros. We are quiet, but we are smart. All the love people pour onto animals, we do not really need, but we know that it teaches people how to love. This is our job, to help people feel love, so we are very happy to be a love mirror for people. We send love back to people, but very few are open enough or loving enough of themselves to feel it. But we continue to send you love, as you are me, and I am you. So really, to love Tocho, is to love

yourself, but the self-judging and self-doubt gets in the way. Now, people must take this love they send to us, and send it to themselves, too. People have a great capacity for self-love and for truly loving themselves. I hope they hear the words from Tocho.

These are my words for all people: Love yourselves truly, so you can love all truly. Thank you for asking me my words for people and giving me the chance to help them.

–CM

Harley
Photo by Noel Breen

TOMASITA, CAT, FEMALE (SPIRIT)

Hi. I really enjoyed life as a cat, even though I wandered and got killed. Of course, I didn't really get killed, just my cat body did. Did you know you never die, just go from body to pure spirit and back?
Enjoy both! Body has advantages, as does spirit. In body, you can touch, taste and smell. Spirit can touch, but most often the recipient doesn't realize it happens. We can do it like a breeze, and can also be felt by someone who is ready. And it can be awesome, I'm told, for someone in body to feel a spirit touch. Just be open to it. Maybe I'll touch YOU!   –W

TRAVELER, BURRO, GELDING

Life is a Journey, and I am the ultimate traveler to guide you. People believe that a journey has a beginning, a middle, and an end. But I pose a question: What if it has a middle, an end, then another middle, then a side, then a top, then a beginning, then a bottom? I have fooled you into thinking about time in a different way by suggesting dimension.
I pose another question: Is time linear? Linear implies a straight line, but there are no straight lines in the universe. A line, by its nature, curves. If this line travels far enough, will it meet itself? Perhaps from each point on the line, time expands out in all directions. All time, therefore, exists simultaneously. There is no past, no present, no future. There is only now. So, you see, one can never be late! I hope that I have given you something to think about."   –CM

TREASURE, HORSE, MARE

Oh, well, thanks for asking me. I'm fairly new here, but I've sure seen a lot in my years. It's so nice to be accepted for who I am!
You know, all of us have control issues to some extent, but it does seem to me that humans have more than others. I wonder why they seem to want to decide everything for others?
For me, if I just concentrate on myself, I have plenty to do. It's OK to desire someone to do this or that, but it's really up to them what they want to do. And, yes, sometimes there have to be rules for everyone's safety, but only for safety, I think. I don't want to control you. I hope you don't want to control me, either.   –W

TREE CHILD, BURRO, JENNY

I have been waiting.

I have been on this planet for quite some time now. I have viewed much of what they do, much of what they think, much of what they feel, and much of what they hide from themselves.

Humans are an interesting study. I prefer not to get too close to them, save some kind, gentle humans that I know. Humans do not understand the effect they have on everything around them. Their actions, their thoughts, their feelings, their hiding from themselves. Yes, they do hide from themselves often. It is as if humans are afraid to accept themselves, accept their true natures, and accept the heart of themselves. They hide their hearts and their true feelings from others, so they can't help but hide their true feelings from themselves.

I am puzzled by this. Why would one hide from oneself? Why would one hide true feelings from oneself? It is a puzzle to me. We (burros) do not hide who we are from each other. We certainly do not hide our true selves from ourselves. This is nonsensical to us. All are on this planet for a reason. For an individual reason and for reasons that benefit the whole (everyone). One cannot possibly achieve anything by hiding feelings and thoughts from oneself.

It appears some humans are split in two. One side for what they are afraid of, the other side hiding that first side from their viewpoint. They believe

that if they looked at their fear side that they would not be able to continue. But the opposite is exactly the case.

Bring together all parts of yourself humans. Bring together all the fear, pain and harsh thoughts you have about yourself and others. Don't hide it. Accept it. By accepting it, it will disappear. You will then understand that those hidden parts of yourself were not real in the first place.

That is all. Thank you for this opportunity.   –SM

Photo by Deb Derr

TRUDIE, HORSE, MARE

Hello, of course, I'll talk to you. Well, it's early – you must get up early too. Lots to see, feel and smell. Sometimes I can smell the start of day, the life, the earth, the joy, the sadness around. Not much sadness though, mostly joy and peace. Humans have that you know – all three senses. There's a lot of joy around here – a lot of hot too.

I love the smells of hay, grass, food, and the smell of water. I feel good, a lot of lazy and happy. Humans try so hard here to make us happy and full of good stuff. We get plenty to eat and good feelings. There's something else in the air too – sometimes sad comes through like hunger, but not hunger just something. I can't name it (yearning).

The humans here are happy we're here, they like us. There's one I need to care for here, one I love a lot (smaller animal). My life is good, my life is free. And that's all I have to say. I'm thirsty, going to drink now. Bye.   –LT

TULIP, DOG, FEMALE

Ahhaaaa (laughing). Humans! They are crazy aren't they? They make me laugh. Laughing is good for the heart and the body. Laughing is good for the mind and the soul. They are so funny. We (dogs and animals) get a kick out of watching them. We know they love us, but sometimes they are crazy. They walk around cleaning, cleaning, cleaning. Picking up what the animals have removed from their bodies. They walk around, feeding, feeding, feeding. Sometimes they sing to themselves. We like that. Sometimes their minds are running off somewhere. We don't like that so much. Sometimes they love us up (touch, snuggle, pet). We love that. There are many of us here so each needs attention. We are a big family and are a lot of work. Why do you think they (these humans) decided on such a big family?

Sue: *They love you all and want everyone to have the best home they can provide. That is why.*

Oh, yes, I know that. But why do they want that? What is it that sustains them?

Sue: *Their love for all of you sustains them, Tulip. They love you all so much that they want good lives for you. It is in their hearts to care for*

such a big family.
Yes, I know that too. Hmmm (thinking). Well, why aren't they with us all the time?
Sue: *What do you mean, Tulip?*
Well, their bodies are here but they are not with us all the time.
Sue: *Do you mean that their minds are elsewhere?*
Yes. If they wanted such a big family, tell them to be with us. Tell them to be more and not do so much. Tell them their be-ing-ness will sustain them. And it sustains us too.
I think that's enough for them to chew on for now (laughing).

–SM

TUXEDO, HORSE, GELDING

I'd like to talk to you about the importance of shoes. Not the kind for riding in, but the kind for walking in. You know that saying about walking in another's shoes? It's true. Having been in another's' shoes lets you roam where they roam and be where they've been.
I would not like to walk in human shoes, although that would give me your perspective.
I am grateful to be here at Hacienda, for I have seen the shoes of many. The donkeys have feet and each marks their own story or trail. Some have wild feet, others like myself have the domestic variety. I like my shoes (hooves) worn low to the ground where I can stamp in a muddle puddle (if one were had).
The importance of shoes goes like this—for every shoe you lose, you gain another, and a new perspective.
Shoes are like trails, they get you where you need to go. We all come in different sized feet and your own would not fit in mine nor would mine with in yours and yet the common ground is there- right below our feet. We walk on it, right? Together, though apart.
You stand in your shoes and I stand in mine. Don't judge another's shoes as they may have been the soul purpose in getting the being to where they stand now. They are not a namesake- but a tool to rig us forward. Thank them, the souls (not soles) of our feet for getting us where we must travel.

–DT

UNCLE WYLDE, BURRO, JACK

Since this goes in a book, I won't talk about anything personal to anyone else. And you know who you are. Aw, I'll just tell you what a rich heritage you come from. Everybody does but each one of us thinks a whole lot more of OUR heritage because it's one thing we can say is really ours. Handed down special for us. You know how it is. I knew a man one time who really thought he owned his burro. He had a lot to learn because that burro had his own ideas of how to get there and when. He had a lot to learn about living with others. I don't know if he learned a lot after all was said and done or if he just kept fighting it. That burro was me. That man died. So I guess he did learn something. It was kind of odd living with him. He talked to himself a whole lot. I would have enjoyed it if he'd have talked to me like that. But I listened in. He couldn't carry a tune but it made him laugh. I think he was missing a bucket or two. I realized living with him that it might not be the ideal life but it sure gave me cause to check in with myself a lot. I wasn't so bad off after all. I really did know more than I thought. And I was quite happy being with myself. Self solitude is part of your

heritage too.

It's good to be with you and your doll. You sure have quite a lot on your hands but I'm glad to see you love it like you do.

–JG

Peanut:
Photo By
Noel Breen

VALENTINE, BURRO, JENNY

People need to be aware. It's amazing how much is missed by an unobservant human. Beauty is everywhere. It doesn't only lie in man-made things. Nature herself is a great artist. Appreciate her work.
Be reasonable. People spend too much time on foolish fancies.

–TC

Photo By
Noel Breen

VALERIE, BURRO, JENNY

Can I talk about truth? I know others have already mentioned it and I don't want to take away from them.
Well, truth makes me free from poverty or bondage. Truth takes away from me the thought of limitation. Everything that is desirable must be a spiritual idea and I know that I have this idea right in my very own mind. This is truth for me. I always have this idea of abundance. Because it is truth for me, I am abundance. You just have to decide if it is truth for you too.

–JG

VELVET MARIE, BURRO, JENNY

I'm Velvet here. This book amazes me and I hope it does you also. I have not been an animal being as long as some here. I was a people also. The difference is, we as animal beings are forgiving, patient and nurturing towards all things. There is a way about everything and we just accept it. All else that people worry about would take care of itself if only you would accept the path, the Journey and your Life. It is after all, up to you.

–S

VICTOR JAMES, HINNY, MALE

Thank you for asking, my old man friend. What shall I talk about, what shall I share? I hope that by sharing what this place means to me, and why, that others may re-think how they treat the beings that live with them. I'm very fortunate. My long-term friend and companion, who chose the name Jewell came here with me and is still with me, and I am very grateful for that. Now we share our space with Flower and Song, who are also very wise, sweet and gentle. Here we don't have to work, just be.

Jewell and I worked very hard until late in life, so this new life here is very welcome. I enjoy so much watching our humans care for all of us. It is different than what we experienced most lives as animals. Just imagine, being loved and accepted for who we are, not what we do for them. Someday that will be how all are treated! We don't mind work, but we do mind just being kept so long as we are able to work. That doesn't seem as if we matter if that is all someone wants us for. I'm slow these days, and that is just fine with everyone here. They don't want me or anyone else here to suffer, and I don't.

Isn't life grand!

–W

VIOLET, DOG, FEMALE

By golly, you are great! I have had so many experiences with humans. I won't tell you how because you won't believe me. I know it all from the inside out.

Humans are the caretakers of life. And humans fumble at it because it is such a big responsibility. Such a great responsibility. Angels guide you. Ask them for help. I do. I ask for help. I get help. Sometimes I have to do it alone, but someone is always there with me.

Do you know about angels? They are all around you. On your shoulder. On your bed watching over you as you sleep.

Ask your children where they are. They know. Children see angels. We see angels, because we are like children sometimes. We grow up and are still children in our hearts, and even sometimes because we have to have human leaders.

You are your own leaders. Sometimes let your children lead you. They will lead you to the angels. Sometimes let us lead you. We will lead you to the angels.

Angels are plentiful. Some of you and some of us become angels when we die. You might find your friends and family there with the angels.

They only have one requirement; that you come to them with love in your heart. No matter how sad you are, no matter how frightened you are, no matter how angry you are. Come to the angels with love.

You can always find one tiny piece of love that hasn't been buried by all those upset feelings. You have it in you. I know you do. You have such love in you that you forget about. Everything you do is from love. Please know that so it guides what you do into loving doings instead of angry doings.

You are made of love like me and everybody who lives. You can find it. Just believe it. Then you will find it, easy.

I know. I am very much in disguise. I know. I am an angel.

–JR

WHISPER, BURRO, JENNY

My, my, my, just when you think everything is going along as you thought it would, life surprises you, right?

Humans always want to know how everything is going to work out. I've noticed that you seem to make lots of "plans." You want to be "in control." I tell you, you're missing all the fun. Every second circumstances change, but your plans are locked in. You're missing opportunities.

Animals remain light on their feet so they can shift and adjust with life's flow. I can't tell you how many times I've found myself facing the other way and thinking I could have missed this wonderful moment if I'd narrowed my focus to a "plan" working out a certain way.

Light on My Feet, by Whisper

As things shift in a way you do not want, look for the clue in the shift. You are being nudged to something even better and more in alignment with who you are and what you truly need. What you think you want may not be truly what will bring you the greatest joy and fulfillment. Remember, light on the feet, light on the feet.

I am grateful for all of life's surprises. They are really gifts. They are showing you what you almost missed - Christina Montana

–CM

WILLIAM, BURRO, JACK AND ANDREW, BURRO, JACK

We are learning to feel happiness and peace as we have never known before. Tell people to never give up. Happiness is just up ahead when all seems dark.   –CM

Photo By Noel Breen

WILLIE-TOO, BURRO, GELDING

I'd like to talk to humans about a practice that occurs in animal sanctuaries. That relates to having babies or children.

We understand and appreciate that you often feel that births should be prevented because of what you perceive as preventing over-crowding. Where will the others who need a home go, you ask, if we allow babies? How would you feel if someone told humans that there are too many of you, so no more new babies? I think you'd object, and we understand why. Of course, crowding can occur, but we do with less space than you might think, especially when the herd has babies sometimes.

Babies are the breath of newness. They are absolutely essential to the good mental health of a herd and all animals. We of the burro family all raise the young. It truly takes a herd, and we also wish to point out that the babies need a herd to do best, and please do not remove a baby from its mother or its herd. If you must, wait at least a year or two. There is much to learn, and that takes time. Would you separate human mother and child at a young age? We don't understand why humans seem to live with such a small part of their family. It was not always so. Is that part of your hurry up life? Please, if you want to help and protect, consider all the wants and needs of those you care for. Thank you!

–W

Willie-Too with Cinnamon, photo by Deb Derr

WYNNE JR., BURRO, GELDING

Animals are not gifts. We are not meant to be thrown overboard, but instead to relish the sun's waves on our backs and sniff the dirt and claw at the ground with our feet. The whole part of my being is ever present in the now and I speak from the now.

When I was born, time was like an angel birthing me into being, and yet I am ancient and old on the spirit plane. I have tramped this ground many times before. I have been as wild as the wild bull in a life. I have been free on the plains (he's talking about a past life as a wild bull) . Today I come to you fully clothed in the shape of the community (burro community) because this is where I can do my greatest good. I have been here before in this clothing, many times.

The knowledge I bring caters to those willing to listen. It is hard for me to speak, as my utter being finds words insurmountable in accuracy. I wish to show you what freedom is. To truly be yourselves in a way that releases all embellishments of you WANT to be.

Animals are so honest. We don't harbor masks. We don't trade in one mask face for another as suits our will. Other beings do that, but not we.

The thing about the mountains and the plains is open space. The freedom to grow. And the fact that being isolated with your own kind has wonders in and of itself. We have elders too, when wild out on the plains. We have those that reassure and offer comfort. But together we stand whole and firm, living a truly full life because of it.

The sky is beautiful here. The rain clouds shed welcome relief. I am blessed. I come forth again and here I light, to begin again in a new incarnation. I am young, but my years go before me like water from an overflowing well. I will offer much nourishment when wealth of knowledge is asked for.

–DT

YANA, HORSE, MARE

Count yourselves lucky for having human hands. I appreciate my hooves and am proud of my feet and how I can utilize them. Your hands are marvelous works of art you can manipulate objects with. Go ahead and paint a pretty picture. People need to utilize their time better in making objects of beauty and desire as then our world will be more beautiful.

We animals lack the appendages you have, but we make beauty in our own way. By marking trees, snaking along the ground, leaving dents in wood, chewing on trees, making hoof stamps and many other prints or markers. These are the signs of life. Of life lived and expressed.

Make good expressions with your hands, dear friends. You deserve to do more than some of you have done. Some people never make a pretty picture in there life, I worry. I want to see people paint and dollop and apply goodness to the hearts of many. Paint a pretty picture. Add beauty to the world.

Your good works are pretty pictures as is a painting itself. If we all made beauty (and the animals are already doing it), then our world will be shinier and more fulfilling for all involved.

I am Yana, a healer in my own right and a maker of prints in the ground. I make my mark with every step. I appreciate the ground absorbing the print and ask that you put your hand in the soil beside mine. This symbolizes us, humans and equines alike, making beauty in our world. Side by side. On equal ground. Literally and figuratively.

People need to be more expressive with the works, deeds, desires they put forth. Laugh, smile and be playful. The expressions (marks in life) you leave behind will be more beautiful to look at and will beautify all of life in a more robust manner.

Enjoy your stay, earthlings. I will enjoy mine. My feet are already marked in the sand with the marks of my herd mates. Do join me in beautifying the world.

Danielle: *Is there anything else you'd like to share?*

Humans are my friends. They have helped me out of a few messes and have helped me on my way in coming here. I am a beautiful bay and a lover of humans. I'm sweet and good tempered. I carry goodness within my soul for all to see.

Sometimes we horses get run down upon and left behind or forgotten like baggage. I don't blame all humans. Life takes us (me and all of you) on different roads. I never forsaw myself coming here. It is a good place. Many people to neck rub. I am happy. I feel safe. I am trustworthy and a doll. Many people like me. Thank you for taking me, Hacienda.

–DT

ZACKARIA, BURRO, GELDING

I would like them to understand that we are of the same stuff. We come from the same mother (earth), the same father (spirit), the same. Our hooves beat on the same ground, we breathe the same fresh air, and we love the same. Our differences are not so different.

Humans, we are alike, you and I. Do we both not want to live and be free?

–SM

ZEKE, MULE, GELDING

Wake up every morning looking forward to the day for every second is special and well worth the effort. Me, I'm constantly amazed at how the little things I notice make up for a very full and enjoyable day.

Count all the little things and you'll live a full and happy life. Me, that is what I do and I have lived a wondrous life. Do you see? Living is in the little things.

Zeke, a "big" mule who lives "little."

–CM

ZORRA, HORSE, MARE

All animals everywhere know of this project, and we are so thankful to participate. Even those who are not participating know it will soon be shared with all humans. From my heart to all human hearts, we are one. We are grateful to those human hearts that are open to who we are, and also to those who are awakening to the fact that we are all one. The New World has begun, a world where love is, and fear is not. A world where all can speak and listen to all beings, without words, regardless of physical body, regardless of where the other being is, and with all spirits regardless of where that spirit is in the universe. Please re-connect with your ability to communicate as the ones are who gather these messages from us do. You are all created with the ability to do it.

Everything has soul/spirit. We on Earth are all of the Earth, part of the Earth. She is our Mother/Grandmother, and we must all love her and take care of her.

Yes, we do have birth mothers, too, and they are also children of the Earth. I'd like you to consider that living with less things, no more than you really need and use, could go a very long way to heal Mother Earth. If you can see what wonder exists in the real world, the world

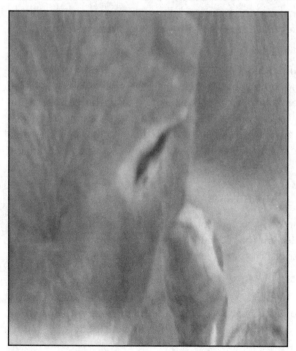

of nature, you might not want so much. Do you need beauty? It is all around you. Do you need to be entertained, go into nature and watch the birds, and trees and animals play.

Embrace the new world. Live in unconditional love. I love you unconditionally. Thank you for hearing my message.

–W

Photo By Noel Breen

ABOUT THE ANIMAL COMMUNICATORS

Anne Angelo, LCSW
914-714-3965 • poweroftheanimals.com
As an animal communicator, my greatest joy is to give animals an opportunity to be heard, as well as providing others with the chance to connect with their own ability to communicate with the animals. I utilize my background as a therapist to enhance the communication process, as well as to aid the healing process related to grief issues and other experiences that might arise during animal communication sessions.

Lyn Benedict - Butte, MT
406-494-5015
Lynn has been a professional animal communicator since 1998. She also does shamanic journeys for animals.

Carolyn Bjur - Chicago, IL
847-543-1450 • carolynbjur@yahoo.com
Carolyn resides in the Chicago area and has been practicing animal communication since 2001. She has studied under a number of spiritual teachers, including Penelope Smith, Carla Meeske and Dr. Kim Ogden-Avrutik.

Tara Caughlan - San Mateo, CA
Tara has been interested in animal communication since she read Kinship with All Life by J. Allen Boone at age 12. Since then, she has put her self-taught skills to use while visiting wild mustangs in Nevada, who have allowed her to approach and touch them. She also practices her animal communication skills while working with wildlife and cats at her local humane society, and enjoys writing about her experiences.

Carole Dennis - New York
585-398-7723 • voicesfortheanimals.com
Carole's lifelong love of animals has taken on a deeper meaning as her awareness of the messages they have to convey continues to open her heart. It is with deep gratitude that she shares this ability with all who come to her seeking a deeper connection with their animal companions. Carole also uses Reiki and essential oils to help animals with health or emotional issues. She currently lives in Upstate New York and is available for consultations.

Janice Gilligan - Shorewood, IL
creaturesconnecting.com
Jan finds communication with animals to be a profound and humbling experience. Located in Illinois, she has provided remote consultations with clients throughout the country and abroad via emailed transcripts.

Janice Goff
Janice and her husband live in the high desert of Arizona. She is co-owner and operator of their family business as plumbing contractors. Her family includes two Australian Shepherds, two cats, a pond full of gold fish and a giant desert centipede.

Barbara Synder Goldberg - Ossining, New York
914-224-4926 • saddleup51@aol.com
Animal Communicator, Certified Flower Essence Practitioner, Reiki Master, Karuna® Reiki Master

Lori Klein
516-216-1126
Animal communication work (studied with Dawn Hayman), Intuitive Energy Healer, Reiki Master/Teacher, Pet Reiki Therapy, Interfaith Minister.

Woni~Dian: Dian Woni Lea
503-704-2246 • starwolfweavings.wolfdancer.org
I have been mentored by several human teachers over the years, but by far the best teachers I have ever met are of the animal kingdom. I live on an acre of fenced land in a yurt, with my three wolfdogs in rural county of NW Oregon. I have become the Nana who walks with "wolves."

Renee Krolo - Chicago, IL
lilabbysam@yahoo.com

Robin Lott
robinlott7@gmail.com

Sue Manley - British Columbia
604-542-1033 • caretolisten.ca
Professional Animal Communicator and Medical Intuitive serving clients in person and at a distance throughout Canada and the U.S. since 1996. Sue's mission is to bring animals and their people together in understanding with the goal of improving both their lives through consultation, problem solving and the opportunity to have a heart to heart.

Melody Mareci
Melody8909@aol.com

Christina Montana - Virginia
540-659-6382 • bigskyspirit.com
Animal Communicator & Shamanic Healer. Christina is committed to making animals' lives happier through enhanced communication. She specializes in healing emotional and physical trauma to return animals to wholeness.

Jeri Ryan, Ph.D - Oakland, CA
510-532-5800 • critterconsultant.com • assisianimals.org
Dr. Ryan has practiced animal communication for 25 years. Her training and experience as a psychotherapist have played a strong role in developing empathic strategies for counseling and problem solving with the animals and their persons. Dr. Ryan founded Assisi International Animal Institute in October 1996. The goal of Assisi is to promote the wellbeing of animals through education and enhancement of the relationships between the animals and their persons. That goal is met also through animal communication workshops facilitated by Dr. Ryan all over the United States, Canada and Europe.

Seneca: Deborah Derr, D.C.
406-222-7982 • draftrescue.com • uilfinearts.redbubble.com
Deb resides in Livingston, Montana. Founder of United in Light, Draft Horse Sanctuary. Deborah is a Chiropractor, Reiki Master and Shaman, living her life nestled amongst the mountains and sharing life with the animals. My life's purpose? Is through God's love and light, to guide and empower all beings in their connection with Source.

Carol Schultz
815-531-2850 • carolschultz.com • animalspiritnetwork.com
Carol Schultz is a professional Animal Communicator and Healer, serving clients throughout her home state of Illinois and across the United States. With a passion to educate, inspire, empower and collaborate, Carol founded Animal Spirit Healing & Education® Network in 2006, an online university and community that offers classes and certificate programs in holistic animal care and intuitive healing arts.

Laila Tisdale - St. Louis, MO
314-332-3454

Danielle Tremblay
303-284-9258 • Whitelightconnection.com
Danielle has been communicating with animals in person and at a distance professionally since 2006. Her greatest joys are working with clients in helping them open their own awareness to hearing the animals themselves through workshops and in personal sessions with the client's own animals. Danielle currently resides in Colorado with her four feline family members and two red eared slider turtles.

Cathy Wells - Shelburne, VT
802-985-2304 • commonheart.net
I've been an animal communicator and holistic mentor for humans and their animals for over eight years. I currently live in Vermont with four English Shire Draft horses which we work daily on a farm, two Shiloh Shepherds who are therapy dogs for kids and senior citizens, two barn cats, two indoor cats and five chickens. They all keep me humble and filled with joy and gratitude for the abundance we share on this earth.

Wynnee: W. Wynne Zaugg - Chino Valley, AZ
928-636-5348 • hdlmsanctuary.org
Co-founder and Executive Director of Hacienda de los Milagros, the teaching and healing animal sanctuary where the beings whose words of wisdom are included in this book reside, or did reside in body. These are my brothers and sisters. Wynne does not offer communication services to the public at this time.

ABOUT HACIENDA DE LOS MILAGROS

Hacienda de los Milagros (HDLM) was originally founded as a retirement home for horses in need in 1990 in Glendale, AZ by W. Wynne Zaugg and Barbara Metzger. "The first horses were boarded, and we were there three times a day, seven days a week taking care of them. In 1993, we moved to our current location with more room that we thought we'd ever use. The first burro arrived in 1995, then the first eight burros we took that had been removed by the Parks Service in Death Valley arrived in 1996, and we soon found out how we'd use the 'extra' space! " By 2009, HDLM had become lifetime home for 39 horses, 139 burros, four mules, three ponies, two hinnies, two mini horses, two llamas, 62 rabbits, four dogs, and some 10-15 cats, most of whom are feral.In 2009, two events happened that changed the direction of HDLM: the economy, and the desire of many of the residents to go forth into the world of humans to teach, heal and spread their unconditional love. "These incredible beings, who had come to us fearful and in need of considerable healing, were now ready to go into the world and spread what they found here. Executive Director Wynne Zaugg says "My family is going on to their greater mission, and I am very proud of them. Some of them I will not see again in this lifetime, and yet the connection will never be severed. We've been together before, and will again. The circle goes on and on."

EXPANDED VISION

HDLM's plans for the future includes our resident faculty of teachers and healers in an expanded educational outreach, extended care facilities and hospice for people who do not wish to leave their best friends behind during their extended stay for medical treatments and their final segment of this lifetime, places to stay for people who wish to do their own healing with the animal residents, a village for humans of all ages to live and a school where human students will get top-level legally required courses, spend time with the animal residents, and be exposed to practitioners of all the major spiritual cultures in the world, so they will understand and treat with respect all these various cultures while choosing their own beliefs for themselves. We believe this is essential for true world peace. Students will re-learn telepathic communication with all life, an ability we are all born with, but soon lose as we take our adult places in the world.

Timing of the steps to implement the full plans will depend, of course, on generosity of humans and business and foundations who share this Vision. This Vision has been communicated to us by the sanctuary residents themselves as an important way to heal the earth and all on it.

PERSONAL GROWTH PROGRAMS

We see a day when we can offer programs to allow two-leggeds who come and visit as well the same opportunities we afford our animal friends. Whether sanctuary residents or wild animals that share their homeland with us, we feel this is a huge step in the healing process of humankind, allowing reconnection with nature and all its inhabitants.

Always being respectful that this is the animals' home, we allow the animals to decide how much human touch they want. We aim to then take the human-animal bond a step further and offer workshops and seminars in animal welfare and communication, and alternative therapies.

We feel this offering is limitless, including programs to further foster the human-non-human animal bond via education vehicles such as human/animal hiking, and other special on the ground programs; that facilitate healing for differently-abled folks. There is no limit to the kinds of interaction that will facilitate teaching and healing.

CHILDREN'S PROGRAMS

HDLM is setting the ground work by planning the development of a residential day-school for children of all persuasions. We will be licensed by appropriate authorities, offer all required courses, and integrated experiential learning agendas beyond mainstream education. Our focus will be to expand educational programs to envelope many cultures from around the world, and to ultimately teach respect and understanding of multiple paths. Our emphasis will be on the value of small class size, close relationships between students and educators (two and four footed) with a true sense of community and growth and expansion of knowledge. We will offer basics in as many of the world's spiritual paths as possible, and as often as possible from people who live those spiritual ways. Our intent will be to graduate students who are open and respectful to all the cultures of the earth, human and otherwise, and will still be able to function as contributing members of whatever society they ultimately reside.

HOSPICE PROGRAMS

We envision a formal program which offers assistance for hospice individuals who are entering the final states of this leg of their journey and have companion animals they do not want to leave. Their companion animals will come with them, and be provided lifetime sanctuary as well.

All this will require significant funding and staffing, and the timing of it will depend on funding and staffing.

IN SUMMARY

We are very excited about the future of Hacienda De Los Milagros. It is not just two-leggeds that would like to offer the world a place to find peace and healing for all living things, but our four legged resident teachers, as well.

Thank you for letting us share this vision with you. Won't you please participate in this journey with us? You can make a difference.

   For the love of all creatures,

     The Milagros